'I'm Nobody Special'

The Story of WVU Football Coach Don Nehlen

By Bill Smith

ISBN 0-934750-51-3

"I'm Nobody Special"
Copyright 1984
Jalamap Publications
Offices: 601 "D" Street
  South Charleston, WV 25303

1277 South Broad Street
Summersville, WV 26651

To Pappy

Foreword

Don Nehlen explained the reason why he was pleased with the title 'I'm Nobody Special' for this book. He said, "Cause I'm not special. I'm just an average guy, a guy who hopefully can laugh at himself. Hey, I'm just a person who's 5-11 inches tall and weighs 178 pounds. I've got light brown hair that bleaches in the sun. I've got green eyes. And I've got a double chin. What's special about that?

"Now I do not think I'm an average football coach."

Michigan Head Coach Bo Schembechler coached Nehlen when Nehlen was a college quarterback and had him as an assistant coach on his staff for three years at Michigan.

Schembechler said, "There was always something special about Don Nehlen. I can remember him as a little, spindly-legged quarterback at Bowling Green State University. He was small, but there was a special quality about him. He just had average talent, but he was intelligent, fiesty, tough, and was a leader. And he was one of the most enthusiastic guys I've ever been around.

"Don has always been a person who genuinely cares about other people. He loves people.

"I considered it a real coup for me when he resigned his job as head coach at Bowling Green and I was able to hire him on my staff. Bowling Green made a big mistake in letting him get away, because he has a great football mind and an excellent capacity to motivate people. And those are two qualities a head coach must have.

"While Don Nehlen was on my staff, he could read my mind like a book. I wish I could have kept him here forever. But I knew it was just a matter of time until I lost him."

Bobby Bowden, the former West Virginia coach, now the head coach at Florida State, said of Nehlen, "He has done a special job of coaching. I thought he did the best job of coaching in the country in 1982, but I thought the same thing about the job he did the year before."

Penn State Coach Joe Paterno said, "Nehlen has done an intelligent job of organizing and coaching at West Virginia University. People talk about what has caused the sudden success of the Mountaineers. Nehlen is the cause of it.

"He's done an excellent job. I'm impressed with how well coached his teams are. They play with great poise and emotion. And they will get better, because the program is solid. I think our dominance of West Virginia is over."

Barry Switzer, Oklahoma head coach said after Nehlen's Mountaineers upset his Sooners, 41-27, to open the 1982 season, "The coaching staff at West Virginia is so much better than it used to be. There is a new coaching philosophy. When we played them I expected a tough game. But West Virginia was excellent the day we played them. I didn't think any one could score 41 points on us, especially West Virginia. But the day we played the Mountaineers, they could have beaten anybody in the country."

Veteran Morgantown sportswriter Tony Constantine, who has seen and covered West Virginia University football games since 1919, said, "There is no question that Don Nehlen has the special quality of getting his players to over achieve, to play better than they are. He certainly has done wonders at West Virginia."

Mickey Furfari, Morgantown *Dominion-Post* executive sports editor, said, "Nehlen is probably the best total coach West Virginia has ever had. He has the qualities for organization and leadership, and knows how to go about it in the proper way. He has instilled a winning attitude in the program from top to bottom. You'd have to be an idiot not to be aware of that."

West Virginia Governor Jay Rockefeller said, "Don Nehlen is a truly extraordinary person. There is something about him, a charisma, a sincerity, a loyalty, a feeling that you know he's going to succeed. He has changed the attitude at West Virginia. The old attitude seemed to be that the players hoped they would win, but assumed they were going to lose. Now, they assume they are going to win.

"His skills range over many areas, which are common to other aspects of life. If he wanted to run for public office, I suspect he would probably do pretty well.

"I love the man."

WVU President E. Gordon Gee said, "My first impression of Don Nehlen was that he was a man of character and integrity. He understands where his life is and where his priorities are. And interestingly enough, my impression of the man is higher today than when I first met him. Generally, I think most sports figures have huge egos. I don't detect that in Nehlen. Quite the contrary, he's too self-effacing.

"If he ever wants to change jobs, I'll bring him over here to organize the university. He's incredibly organized.

"Before Don Nehlen came to West Virginia, I was not a football fan. I have become one. No, I'll phrase that another way. I became a fan of Don Nehlen's and then I became a football fan. He's a special person."

Phil Villapiano, 13-year veteran linebacker with the Oakland Raiders and Buffalo Bills and a member of the 1976 Super Bowl champion Raiders, said, "When I played for Coach Nehlen at Bowling Green, I caused him all kinds of problems. He bailed me out of trouble quite a few times. But he mentally prepared me for professional football. If it hadn't been for him I don't think I would have played in four Pro Bowls. I remember he'd grab me and say, 'Phil, you can be a pro.'

"I feel like I owe everything I have today to Don Nehlen.

"He took a genuine interest in every player who played for him. He'd have the players out to his house to eat. I used to look forward to going to his house and eating Merry Ann's (Nehlen's wife) mashed potatoes and gravy.

"I played for John Madden at Oakland and he had the same relationship with his players. There is a lot of John Madden in Don Nehlen.

Mark Miller, Bowling Green assistant coach and quarterback under Nehlen when Nehlen coached at Bowling Green, said, "Coach Nehlen was always so enthusiastic and always had special little ways of motivating you. He was the kind of coach who would have you over to his house on Sunday. He really cared about his players. As a player I always knew I came first with him."

Former WVU quarterback Jeff Hostetler, who is now Nehlen's son-in-law, said, "Coach Nehlen is the most fired up person when he is coaching that I've ever been around. During the season football consumes him. His enthusiasm carries over to his players. And the most important thing about that enthusiasm is that he always seems to have a lot of fun when he's coaching. Consequently, his players have fun.

"I can remember a few times when we'd be out practicing in the cold and snow and he'd say, 'Men, this is a great day for football, just a great day for football.' Sometimes I'd look at him and think, 'How can this man enjoy football all the time?'

"But I think that's what makes him a great coach. He always has that enthusiasm for the game.

"And the thing the players respect him most for is that he's honest with them. His players always know where they stand with him. But he never tries to impress them.

"I'll never forget my first meeting with him in his office when I was thinking about transferring to West Virginia from Penn State. The first thing he did was come out from behind his desk, shake my hand and then give me a good solid hit in the chest. It was as if he was saying, 'I'm the coach.'

"Then he grabbed me by both shoulders and said, 'You aren't the best looking guy in the world, but we'd like to have you here.'

I thought, 'Why am I thinking about coming to West Virginia? This guy certainly isn't trying to impress me at all.' But that's just his way. You can't help but respect him.

Houston Oilers' quarterback Oliver Luck, who played for Nehlen's first two WVU teams, said, "He is a different type coach to be around. The one thing he does best is motivate his players. And he does it in a very subtle way. That's a special talent and one Coach Nehlen is a master of. Also, he always keeps a level head. He's not up one week and down the next. He keeps his cool as well as anyone I've ever seen."

Darryl Talley, ex-Mountaineer All-American linebacker now with the Buffalo Bills, said, "Coach Nehlen works on your mind. He believes that football is 90 percent mental and 10 percent physical. And believe me, when he gets through working on your 90 percent, the 10 percent is easy. The way he coaches made everyone on the team want to be in the lineup on fourth down and one."

Former Bowling Green teammate Chuck Perry, Logan, W. Va., native, now vice-chairman, chief executive officer and partner of Golden Bear International, Jack Nicklaus Companies in North Palm Beach, Fla., said, "I'm not surprised that Don Nehlen's West Virginia teams over achieve. He was an over achiever himself. When he played any sport in college he always thought he could win, even when he didn't have a snowball's chance in hell.

"I've known Don since he was a sophomore quarterback at Bowling Green back in 1955. He was a skinny little guy. And I never could understand how such a frail-looking guy could be so tough. He was one tough cookie."

Doyt Perry, former great head coach who coached Nehlen as a player at Bowling Green, said, "Don Nehlen stood out right off the bat as one of the most enthusiastic young men I had ever seen. He was just go-go all the time. I never coached anyone who was more gung-ho than Don. I think if I had told him to stay up all night with his head gear on, he would have done it. He was just that kind of kid."

Lifelong friend Larry Kelly said, "Don's outstanding trait is that he's humble. And it's not put on."

Ken Schoeni, assistant to the athletic director at Bowling Green, has spent many summer vacations with Nehlen. Schoeni said, "Don Nehlen is unique in that he never wants to take advantage of people. For instance, Don and his coaches at West Virginia all get new cars from car dealers. And Don considers that a big plus for his program.

"One time I visited Don in Morgantown. He was having an outing for all his coaches. While they were there, Don went around and inspected all their cars, and he said to a couple of them, "Your cars look awful dirty. It doesn't look to me like you're taking care of them. Let's be getting those cars cleaned up. You know, having a car given to you to drive is a privilege. Don't abuse that privilege.

"But that's Don. He never wants to take advantage of anybody. And to me, that shows the true colors of a person. Don is a stickler for things like that. He also keeps his car cleaner than anyone I've ever seen. He waxes it at least once a week. He'll wash it off before he goes to the office in the morning. Sometimes, he'll even scrub the white wall tires before he goes to work.

"He has always kept his cars spotless. He goes at everything he does the same way."

Bob Marcum, South Carolina athletic director who recommended Nehlen for the West Virginia job, said, "His teams play with emotion because the head coach always runs on 220 current. Nehlen is a self-starter."

Former Cleveland Browns' great Lin Houston, an old

friend of Nehlen's, said, "One year when Don was head coach at Bowling Green, my youngest daughter tried to enroll at Bowling Green, but the fall quota for girls was filled. So, I called Don and asked for his advice.

"He asked, 'Can she go to summer school?'

"I said, 'Yes.'

"And he said, 'Then send her up and I'll get her in on my football quota.'

"And my daughter enrolled at Bowling Green as an unofficial member of the Bowling Green football team. When I thanked Don for what he had done, he said, 'No big deal. I was allowed to bring in 25 walkons. So, I just brought in 24 and one girl. Besides, it wasn't any problem. My wife Merry Ann worked in the registrar's office and some of my best friends worked in the housing department.'

"One of his special attributes has been that he's always willing to offer others a helping hand."

Former WVU assistant coach Gary Tranquill, now head coach at Navy, said, "First and foremost, Don Nehlen is a warm, genuine human being. He's easy to work for because he's always on an even keel. When you meet him for the first time, or the thousandth time, he's always the same. He never changes.

"It takes a special quality to be a successful head coach. I don't know what it is, but I know that Don Nehlen has it."

WVU defensive coordinator Dennis Brown said, "I observed an example of how Don's former players feel about him. It was the year after he resigned at Bowling Green. He and I were both on Bo Schembechler's staff at Michigan.

"For a while that year, it seemed like every morning there would be two or three of his Bowling Green players drive to Michigan to see him. They were having problems adjusting to Denny Stoltz, the coach who succeeded Nehlen at Bowling Green.

"Don would say to the kids, 'You have to go back to Bowling Green. You have a new coach, a new coaching staff and a new system. You have to go back and adapt.'

"It was a special thing. I had never seen a coach's former players flock to the coach for advice like Don's former players did. It told me that he was a player's coach, and that his players loved him."

Russ Jacques, WVU offensive coordinator, said, "I've never known Don to be anything but a perfect gentleman. He's always been straight-arrow, sort of a perfect kind of guy.

"And sometimes, it's kind of scary to be around him."

Jack Harbaugh, head coach at Western Michigan who was an assistant coach at Bowling Green under Nehlen, said, "Don was always obsessed with being successful. He was a tremendous driver, not of other people, but of himself. I always felt he was destined to be a great coach."

Nehlen's favorite sister, Carolyn, said, "Donnie (she has always called him that) would have loved for daddy to have lived to see what he has accomplished. Daddy was so proud of that kid. Daddy would have been in seventh heaven if he could have lived to see Donnie today." (Nehlen's father died in 1972.)

(Editor's Note: In working with Don Nehlen on 'I'm Nobody Special,' Nehlen related a story about a discussion he had with Michigan's Bo Schembechler. Schembechler talked about the time an author wrote a book about him. Nehlen said, "Bo told me he and that author couldn't agree on anything. Bo said they argued all the time about the content of the book."

Nehlen turned to me and asked, "Are we doing something wrong, because we haven't had one disagreement? Or, am I just too easygoing?"

I didn't answer that. But I thought, "No, the word isn't easygoing. The word is special.")

Chapter One

The coaches' meeting room on the second floor of the West Virginia University Coliseum was dark. The door was shut.

Inside, all alone, was the new head football coach of the Mountaineers. He was watching a movie — for a purpose. That purpose was to find out something about his new team. After all, he had just accepted the job and knew nothing about West Virginia — the team, the university, or the state.

The one thing he did know was the Mountaineers had been losers for the last four years and five of the last six. And he knew his job was to change that.

He had just come from one of the most successful football programs in the country — the University of Michigan, where the Wolverines play to crowds of 100,000 plus and annually are up in the polls and go to bowls.

This cold January day, 1980, he set to work. The first order of business was to familiarize himself with his new team.

Football coaches work a good portion of the time with movie projectors. They look at the game films, at scrimmage films, at films of high school prospects, at films of opponents. They look at films until their eyes turn red and their heads ache. They spend hour after hour in darkness with only the flickering light of the projector flashing images of the action on a movie screen.

The projector whirred.

Nehlen was watching a film of the 1979 WVU-Penn State game in front of a crowd of 77,923 at University Park, Pa. It was a game in which the Mountaineers scored first and then lost — as usual — 31-6. As he watched, he knew that Penn State always wore blue and white. Plain blue jerseys, plain white pants and white helmets with a single blue stripe in the middle. On the road the Nittany Lions' uniform was all white. No frills. And they always wore the same color helmet.

The other team flashing on the screen was wearing light-colored helmets. The helmets looked white, too. They were white! There was something on the side of the helmets, too. An unidentifiable glob. At least, that's what it seemed to Nehlen. Actually, it was an outline in the shape of the state of West Virginia with a fancy WVU stuck in the middle of it. And the pants and jerseys the players wore had all kinds of stripes on them — white, gold and blue.

He checked a film from the season before. That year the Mountaineers' helmets were an off-color gold. The stripes on the pants were blue and white.

Nehlen said aloud — to himself, "WHICH TEAM IS MINE?"

"I thought West Virginia's colors were blue and gold. What the heck is this with those light-colored helmets with that crazy configuration on the side and all that white on the sides of the pants? White?"

He immediately turned off the projector and called for equipment man Mike Kerin. "Get rid of those uniforms," he told Kerin. "We're gonna get new uniforms — NOW! And I want uniforms so that when our guys go out on the field there will be no question in anybody's mind as to who we are.

"I want blue and gold. Those are our colors. No stars. No stripes. No frills. I don't want any of that junk on them.

"And I want a solid blue helmet. Solid blue. Deep blue."

The new coach wasn't through yet. He said, "And get rid of that configuration on the sides of those helmets. Nobody can tell what that is. What is it anyway?"

At that moment, the idea of a 'WV' logo began to percolate in Nehlen's mind.

He knew he wanted a new logo for his new team. A new identity. He wanted something that would be simple, striking and easily identifiable, something that could be seen from a distance (hopefully, on a fast-moving object), something that would say 'West Virginia' in no uncertain terms.

The problem was Nehlen was neither an artist nor a graphics man. He knew he wanted something different. He just didn't know what.

He and Kerin sat down with pencil and paper in hand, put their heads together and created several designs — designs with either WV or WVU in them. But the right decision eluded them. It's not that simple to create a new logo that says it all with letters when you've spent most of your life working only with X's and O's.

Nehlen went to assistant athletic director Mike Parsons, then the sports information director, for help. He told him what he had in mind and showed him the sketches.

Parsons said, "I got the idea of what he wanted, but the sketches weren't very good. I knew we had to go to a professional."

Parsons did. He called sports artist John Martin in Kansas City. Martin, the brother of then WVU athletic director Dick Martin, had designed covers for World Series programs, done work for professional football and

1

baseball teams and created sports paintings that hang in the offices of professional clubs all over the country.

Parsons explained what Nehlen wanted and sent Martin the sketches. In a few days Martin called back and said, "You can't use these. You can't put any of those on a helmet. Tell you what I'll do. I'll make a few sketches and send them to you. I might be able to come up with something the coach will like."

Sure enough, in exactly three days the sketches came in the mail. Parsons opened the envelope and there were three. And the one on top was the 'WV.' Parsons said, "As soon as I saw it, I knew that was the one. It stuck out like a sore thumb."

He took the sketches to Nehlen and the coach agreed with Parsons' choice. He said, "That one is dynamite. Let's do it." It was the one . . . the new insignia of the Mountaineers . . . the one that would go on the side of those solid blue helmets . . . the 'WV.'

Nehlen had his logo. A new look for his new team. And, most importantly, West Virginia University had a new coach, one who would guide the destiny of the Mountaineers, make decisions and improve the image of WVU football, not just the uniforms, but the performance as well. Don Nehlen, the guy they used to call "Bonesey" in his hometown of Canton, Ohio, was at the helm.

Chapter Two

The year 1935 was drawing to a close. In a few hours a new year would begin.

It was a cold, snowy New Year's Eve in Canton, Ohio. In the comfortable, tidy frame house on Clarendon Ave., S.W., mother Margaret, everyone called her Marge, was experiencing the first signs of labor pains. She knew the feeling of the contractions. After all, this would be her sixth child.

Four years earlier she had given birth to twin girls, Carol and Carolyn. Four years before that it was a son, Carl, who was always called Sonny. Three years before that it was girl, Dorothy. And three years before that it was another girl, Jane.

The contractions were coming closer together. Marge knew it wouldn't be long. She said to her husband, "Carl, I think we'd better get ready to go the hospital."

Carl, who acquired the nickname "Pappy" after those twins were born, got up from his chair, put on his coat and went out to get the car warmed up. Marge gathered up personal items and bundled up to protect against the cold. Marge was always an independent person.

The ride to Aultman Hospital didn't take long. It was only a few blocks away. Pappy pulled up in front, helped Marge out of the car and up to the hospital area.

Shorly after that the clock struck "twelve." It was 1936. And a few minutes after midnight, Donald Eugene Nehlen was the first New Year's baby boy born in the city of Canton.

There was nothing significant about the event. The baby, who would thereafter be called Donnie by Mom and Dad, sisters, brothers, relatives and old friends, was a scrawny little thing.

The birth certainly didn't rank with other events that had occurred recently, like President Franklin D. Roosevelt sending his social security plan to Congress, or the talk of a boycott of the Berlin Olympics, or Babe Ruth signing a contract to play with the Boston Braves and ending his career as a Yankee, or a player named Jam Berwanger of the University of Chicago being named the best college football player in the land. And it wasn't as important as Stanford playing Southern Methodist University in the Rose Bowl later that same day.

This was just the birth of a baby to a middle-class family in a middle-class neighborhood in a middle-class city. This was the "Great Depression" and the baby was just another mouth to feed.

Pappy made enough at his job as cashier (accountant) for the Automatic Steel Products Company to support his large family. There was no problem in that regard. Pappy knew all about hard work and hard times. His parents had come to this country from Germany. And he had quit school in the eighth grade and gone to work. Later, he resumed his education at a business college. It's just that there wasn't any extra money for extra things.

Mom worked, too, to help support her brood. She always worked, whether to earn extra money, or to keep her home spotless. As she used to say, "Clean enough to eat off the floors."

That left the raising of Donnie to his sisters. And they spoiled him. Mom said he was a "good boy" and "never got into trouble." Jane said, "He was ornery and a little sissy. Why, he sucked on a baby bottle until he was about five years old.

"He'd come up to me, tug on my skirt and say, 'Jane, make me canned milk, water and sugar.'

"He'd suck on that bottle and then hide it behind the couch so people wouldn't know he was such a baby that he had to have a bottle. We were always finding a baby bottle with sour milk in it under the couch."

Big sister didn't always appease him. "I had to bathe the twins and then Donnie," said Jane. "And I didn't particularly care for the job. When I got through with the twins, I'd grab Donnie and shake him and say, 'You little brat, I wish you were old enough to bathe yourself. I don't love you anymore."

"He'd look at me and say, 'I wuv you, Jane.' "

It's tough for a young boy to grow up when he's being mothered by older sisters. The truth is what happened to him can be summed up in a word — spoiled. In fact, Mom worried that he was too much of a baby and held him out of the first grade for a year.

"Mom was just afraid Donnie was a little too much of a baby to start school," Carolyn said. "He was such a skinny little kid."

Donnie may have been slight of build, but he had a competitive nature that was in the embryo stage. He loved the outdoors and was always pleading with Marge and his sisters to let him go out — even in the worst kind of weather.

"I remember one winter," Jane said, "Donnie couldn't have been more than four. He pleaded for us to let him go outside and play in the snow with the other kids. We said, 'No.' He was so little the snow would have been over his head.

"He went to the door, opened it and yelled at the kids playing in our yard, 'I wish you dod-damn kids would go home so I won't have to watch you.' I think he learned that language from sitting around watching mom and dad play poker. They loved to play poker and played it all the time."

Mom, now 80, still attends her poker club a couple of times a month. "Do we play for money?" she said. "Sure. You see anything wrong with that? I used to belong to three poker clubs — until my husband got sick. Then I had to give them up."

Even before he went to school, Donnie was a pretty good penny ante poker player. Carolyn said, "He'd bet on those poker hands like it was life or death. He was a good player then and still is now."

Pappy wasn't an athlete. Oh, he liked to bowl and in Canton circles was known as a good one. In later years, he would take up golf. But he never played sports like football, basketball or baseball. He was too small. Pappy was only 5'6" and never weighed more than 140 pounds soaking wet. Besides, back in the Depression he didn't have time to play.

None of his girls were athletically inclined, either. Neither was Sonny. But that was before Donnie.

After being held out of the first grade for a year, Donnie enrolled at Clarendon Grade School. In the third grade he met a little girl named Merry Ann Chopson, who lived just around the corner on Eighth Street. At that age, Donnie didn't have time for girls, unless they were interested in shooting marbles or playing catch. His interest in Merry Ann would come much later.

Donnie was always playing games. He would go to the upstair bedroom with boyhood friend Dick White, draw a circle on the rug and shoot marbles. White was three years older and used to baby-sit Donnie when their parents ran around together and played cards together. By the time Donnie was a sixth-grader he was the marbles champ of his school and even competed in the city championship.

The baby of the Nehlen family was always a helper, too. He loved to cooperate. Carolyn said, "When Donnie was in grade school . . . oh, maybe the fourth grade, the school would have scrap drives. All the children would collect scrap metal and the school would sell it and make money. Donnie would haul everything he could find around the house that was made of metal. He even took the metal wheels off his bicycle. Once, Mom and Dad bought a new kitchen table to replace our old metal one. They put the old one down in the basement.

"And sure enough, one day I saw him marching down the sidewalk toward school dragging that metal table. I think if our house had been made of metal, he would have tried to dismantle the house and haul it off to school."

Mom had trouble keeping clothesline poles, too. This had nothing to do with shooting marbles. He was also interested in pole vaulting and would take Mom's poles and use them to practice vaulting. He'd take those poles and try time and again to pole vault onto the roof of the garage. He used to drag Mom's poles over to the old Timken farm and vault across the creek that ran through the middle of the property. Mom lost more poles that way. Years later, the Timken farm would become the site of the Pro Football Hall of Fame.

The efforts to vault to the roof of the garage and across the creek paid off because when Donnie was an eighth-grader he competed in his first and only school track meet. "He won the pole vault in the city junior high school meet," said Carolyn. "He was so proud of the ribbon he won for that."

But it was his only experience with track and field. He was too busy running and jumping into other activities to spend much time running and jumping on a track.

In the summers Carolyn, his favorite sister, would pack him a lunch and ne'd head for Meyers Lake and swim all day. Donnie learned to swim at an early age. "It seems as soon as I got around the water I started swimming," Nehlen said: "I was a pretty good swimmer. Good diver, too. Did I go off the high board? Right now, I think I first went off the high board when I was about six years old."

In the winters he would head for the duck pond at City Park and skate on the ice until his ankles "would fall off." He would go down McKinley Monument hill on a pair of skiis, or a pair of skates, at breakneck speed. "It was stupid to go down that hill on a pair of ice skates," he said. "But for some reason I never had any fear. I was always trying something new."

Donnie didn't know it at the time, but the reason he was so competitive in all kinds of sports was because he was so small. He made up for his lack of size by disciplining himself and practicing hour after hour to excel. He never had time for the usual kids' games of tag and hide-and-seek, although he did play kick-the-can, a street version of soccer (although he probably didn't know it at the time).

But at that early age the real loves of his life were baseball and basketball. Football, although he played the usual pickup games in vacant lots and in the streets, didn't figure much in the thinking of this skinny little 90-pounder for obvious reasons.

Donnie got an old beatup glove and ball, and played catch with anyone willing to take the time. He bounced the ball off walls and fielded it. When he wasn't splashing around in Meyers Lake, he was playing ball in dusty vacant lots with the gang. Slowly, but surely, the kid began to get a reputation as fearless fielder — a guy who could scoop up a scorching grounder or a hard shorthop and make it look easy. He helped organize a team and went to the local Ford garage and talked the owner into buying the team T-shirts so the gang would look like a real team.

When he wasn't playing baseball, or swimming, or diving, or skiing, or ice skating, he was shooting a basketball at a hoop in the back of the house. Nehlen said, "My brother put up the basket behind the house we lived in on Broad Avenue. (Pappy had moved the family to a bigger house a few years after Donnie was born.) As I remember, I always played basketball with older kids.

"My twin sisters were four years older than me and their boyfriends used to come over to see them. I played basketball with them out back. It was a pretty big

4

challenge for a grade schooler like me to play with high school guys. No question, it made me work harder and made me better. I think I decided at an early age I wanted to be an athlete. That meant a basketball player in the winter, a baseball player in the summer and a football player in the fall.''

"Although no one in my family was into athletics, I think my interest was natural. Canton has always been a mecca for high school sports. Canton McKinley High School always had great athletic teams. Massillon High School was only 15 miles away. Anyone who knows anything about Ohio high school football knows what great teams Massillon turns out.

"I remember going to Fawcett Stadium (adjacent to McKinley High and the Pro Football Hall of Fame) when McKinley played, and crawling under the fence. I couldn't have been more than 10 years old. I never missed a game on Friday and Saturday nights.

"Didn't have any money, but I'd find a way to get in. Under the fence. Over the fence. Beg a ticket. The whole bit. We knew where the policemen on guard were. I think most of them knew us and just turned their heads when we were sneaking in. Unless it was a big game like McKinley vs. Massillon, I don't think they cared.''

Donnie's real introduction to competitive football didn't come until he enrolled at Canton Lincoln High School. All high schools in Canton were four-year schools and he was a puny little freshman.

It was early September 1950. Freshman football coach George Luther pinned a notice to the school bulletin board announcing that "all freshmen who wish to try out for freshman football are asked to report to the gymnasium this afternoon.''

Little 5'8", 115-pound Donnie reported and sat in the gymnasium balcony with about 65 other freshmen and waited for the coach to issue him a uniform. "I'll never forget that day," he said. "I sat there beside another little guy, Vic DeOrio, who was smaller than I was. Vic was about 5'4" and couldn't have weighed much more than 100 pounds. The coach issued uniforms to everyone, except Vic and me. We were the only two kids left sitting in that balcony who didn't get uniforms.

"The coach told us. 'You guys are just too little.'

"But after a couple days of practice, some of the guys who got uniforms decided football wasn't for them. They turned in their uniforms and we finally got ours. They weren't exactly tailored to fit us. The first football helmet I was issued was so big you could spin it around on my head. I think my pants came down to around my ankles. I know DeOrio's did. Other than that, about the only thing I remember about freshman football was not getting to play and getting splinters from sitting on the bench.''

(Four years later, Nehlen quarterbacked Lincoln to the city championship, made all-county honorable mention, all-Ohio and was voted the outstanding athlete in his school. DeOrio went on to become all-county, all-state and a Little All-American running back in college.)

Donnie's second year of football was worse. He was on what they called the "rat meat" squad. Today coaches call that the scout team, the team that runs plays of the up-coming week's opponent. Also, players on that squad spend more than a little time holding blocking dummies and being dummies who are blocked.

And it was on one October afternoon when the "rat meat" squad was running an opponent's plays that Donnie took a hit, was knocked down and didn't get up. It was his first injury — a broken collarbone.

"I wasn't too happy with my football career at that point," he said. "First of all, the high school basketball coach was mad at me. I was going to be a starter in basketball and now I was sidelined with a broken collarbone." Mom wasn't too happy, either. She wasn't too keen about her youngest son playing such a violent sport anyway.

His shoulder healed and he played basketball. That spring he played baseball. Donnie ended up being a 10-letter winner — Canton Lincoln's first ever. He won four in baseball, three in basketball and three in football. His senior year he was co-captain of the football team, captain of the baseball team and president of the school's Varsity Club.

But there was a tough period in football for him, between his sophomore and junior years. "I was ready to quit," he said. "I wasn't playing. I really couldn't see any future in getting banged around. But two assistant coaches, Bill Doolittle (who later was head coach at Western Michigan) and Jim Whittaker (his brother Bob was head coach at Bowling Green State University), came over to my house and talked with my dad.

"They said, 'We know he's little, but don't let him quit. He has the potential to be a good player.'

"I wasn't sure I believed them. Heck, I was still a skinny little kid. Here I was going to be a junior and still didn't weigh but about 130. I used to eat and drink everything I could to gain weight — milkshakes, two and three breakfasts, mashed potatoes by the ton, sweets, everything. Nothing worked. I was very self-conscious about my size.''

Also, at that point in his life, Donnie thought his future was in basketball and baseball. He was in the starting lineup in those sports. That made a difference. "And I had dreams of being a major league ballplayer some day," he said.

A lot of 16-year-olds dream the same dream. However, Donnie had good reason. He was considered by many the best third baseman in the county. Earl Schreiber, former executive director of the Pro Football Hall of Fame, was then recreation director for the Timken Roller Bearing Company. One of his many duties was to organize the company's baseball team in the Class A industrial league. And he was looking for a third baseman.

Schreiber said, "One day I went to a Lincoln game and saw this skinny kid playing third base. He was a smooth glove man. But he was skinny. Everyone called him 'Bones' and 'Weiner.' After the game I asked him if he'd like to play for the Timken team. I told him I'd get him a summer job in the company's recreation program. And for the next seven years 'Bonesey' was our third baseman.''

Donnie played with such players as Jim Swierczek, former great Marshall University end of the early 1950s, and Vince Costello, former linebacker for the Cleveland Browns. Sweirczek, now a schoolteacher in the Canton area, said, ''I'll never forget the enthusiasm he had. It just oozed out of him. And he was a heckuva fielder and had a rifle arm. Wasn't much with the bat, though. A dead pull hitter with not much power. But he did hit .397 one year, though. That was in 1955 when we won the league championship.''

I'll never forget the day Mr. Schreiber asked me if I wanted to play ball for Timken in the Class A league,'' Nehlen said. ''Then he told me he would give me a summer job. That was like being paid to play baseball. Now, you have to understand, back then that Class A league was big stuff in Canton. They played games every Monday, Wednesday and Friday night. Everybody went to the city parks to see those games. Crowds used to run about 3,000. That was big-time stuff, especially to a 16-year-old.

''When Mr. Schreiber made me that offer, I literally flew home. I was excited. I couldn't wait to tell my dad. That was like dying and going to heaven.''

Schreiber said, ''I singled 'Bonesey' out after watching him and talking to his coaches. He had outstanding ability. He was the best third baseman around. That's what we were looking for. Although the league was made up of older men, he had no trouble fitting in. But he had to have other qualities, especially leadership. It didn't take us long to realize that was one of his stronger qualities. We couldn't have afforded to hire a person in our summer program to supervise the children of our employees if he hadn't been a person of high moral character.

''Bonesey was never a hell-raiser. As far as I know, he never did anything out of line. Oh, he was a boy and enjoyed himself. But he was the kind of person you could rely on. I just felt there was something special about him. And there never was a single moment that I was sorry I put him on our team and hired him in our summer program.''

Nehlen, who at age 16 was considered a major league prospect, became such a fine player in the Class A league that in 1983 he was voted into the Stark County Baseball Hall of Fame.

Meanwhile, Donnie's interest in football picked up again. Thanks to the urging of his high school assistant coaches, he stayed with football. He decided to give it one more try. And lo and behold, he became the starting quarterback his junior year and led Lincoln to a winning record (5-4).

Basketball still held a fascination for him, though. That winter he averaged 10 points on a poor 4-13 team, but one February night he threw in a shot from mid-court at the buzzer to nip rival McKinley 54-53. Beating McKinley was akin to winning a state championship. It didn't happen very often.

''I remember getting the ball and looking at the clock,'' Nehlen said. ''I saw there were only two seconds remaining and I just turned and threw the ball at the basket. It went in.'' The next season, Donnie's senior year,

he averaged 13 points a game and sparked Lincoln to a 13-6 record. In one game against Canton South he made two free throws with 13 seconds to play for a 55-53 win. It was such a rivalry that near the end of the game a spectator came out of the stands and slugged a South player. ''The game was what you would call a slugfest,'' he said.

A pretty young girl named Merry Ann Chopson, the same one Donnie enrolled in the third grade with, was ''Basketball Queen.'' By this time Donnie had noticed girls and was dating her. And he was the one who placed the crown on her head.

It was that year (1953) that Donnie really came into his own in football. On October 9 in front of a crowd of 12,000 at Fawcett Stadium (the one he used to sneak in as a kid), Donnie threw a 31-yard touchdown pass to lead Lincoln past McKinley, 20-14. And five weeks later he fired a 22-yard touchdown pass to lead his team past Canton Timken High School, 39-7. Lincoln finished the season 6-3, but that win clinched the city championship. In Canton in those days a city championship was a big, big thing.

He was named second team all-city and second team all-county. And when asked what he had gained from all the hard work put into that successful season, he said, ''If I gained anything, it sure wasn't weight.''

Malvern Randels, Donnie's high school shop teacher, remembers him very well. He said, ''I was one of those who doubted that he was big enough to play football. How wrong I was! I was the public address announcer for Lincoln football games and Coach Baughman instructed me to add some pounds to Donnie when I announced the starting lineup. He didn't want the opposition to know how small he was. He only weighed about 135 his senior year. I used to announce him at 145.''

Along about that time, Bowling Green State University became interested in him, too, for his leadership qualities.

Bowling Green offered him a three-way scholarship — one-third to play football, one-third to play basketball and one-third to play baseball. ''And that was just for tuition and fees,'' Nehlen said. ''I was going to have to work for my room and board. Colleges back then didn't give you a free ride like they do today.'' Nehlen visited Miami of Ohio, but the coach there then (Ara Parseghian) didn't think he was big enough.

''The prospect of going to college really excited me. I never regarded myself as a great student, but I was a solid one. I made B's and C's. Actually, I was one of those kids who enjoyed school. I looked forward to going to school every day because I couldn't wait for what happened when each school day was over — sports. And now to be offered the chance to go to college and continue playing sports! Well, it was beyond imagination.

''College was never mentioned around my house. My parents didn't have the money to send any of us to college. I'm the only member of my family to ever go to college. The only one. And if it hadn't been for Bowling Green offering me that scholarship, I probably wouldn't have gone. I remember telling my dad about the offer, one-third to play each sport.

6

"Dad said, 'Well, three-thirds makes a whole. You'd better take it.' "

Sister Carloyn disagreed. "Dad would have found the money to send Donnie to college somehow," she said. "I don't think he ever missed a single game that boy ever played — football, basketball or baseball. Dad worshipped the ground Donnie walked on. Donnie could always look up in the stands and know that Dad was there." Dad wouldn't live to see Donnie grow up and be a successful coach. He died in 1972 at age 72 of emphysema.

The summer of 1954 was rapidly approaching. Donnie graduated from Lincoln and wrote in the yearbook his ambition of being "a millionaire . . . a major league ballplayer." And he was looking forward to his usual summer of playing baseball for Timken and working in the company's recreation program, taking care of the ball diamonds, mowing the grass, raking the infields and lining the fields.

That was the summer that Timken employees went on strike. Nehlen said, "Things were tough what with layoffs, the strike and all. Earl (Schreiber) said he wasn't going to be able to hire me because if he took anyone on, it had to be a laid-off employee.

"In high school, I was in what they called the technical course. I had a lot of trigonometry and plain and solid geometry and all that stuff. So, Earl said, 'Bonesey, I'm going to put you in our training program.'

In between my senior year in high school and my freshman year at Bowling Green, I went to school half a day, taking math courses, and worked the other half day, helping design bearings in the engineering department of the company. The people at Timken thought I planned to be an engineer and was going to attend Georgia Tech or the University of Cincinnati on their co-op plan.

"That bothered me because I had already accepted a scholarship to Bowling Green. I had no intention of going to Georgia Tech or Cincinnati. But my boss at Timken didn't know that. I kept up the farce until about July. Then I said to Earl, 'Who's going to tell those people I'm not going to be an engineer? Who's going to tell them I'm going to Bowling Green on an athletic scholarship?'

"Earl said, 'Well, I guess you are. They won't care. Just go in and tell them.'

"I said, 'I don't know about that. My boss has test scores on me. He's talked to me about my future in the company. No sports. Just strictly to college to study to be an engineer.' "

But a few days later, Donnie mustered his courage and did it. Although scared to death, he went into the office of the head of engineering and said, "I'm sorry, sir, but I can't go to Georgia Tech or Cincinnati. I've accepted an athletic scholarship to attend Bowling Green State University and play football, basketball, and baseball."

"When I told him that, he looked at all 135 pounds of me and said, 'You're going to play college football!'

"I said, 'Yes, sir, I'm going to make a stab at it.'

"Well, he almost died laughing."

Chapter Three

The skinny, crewcut kid, the one everyone back home in Canton called "Bones," pulled his "Brown Bomber," that spanking clean 1950 Pontiac his dad had given him, off Ohio Route 25 onto the main drag in the little college town of Bowling Green.

Don Nehlen — he never did like the name Donnie — wasn't exactly your picture of confidence that September day in 1954. Eighteen years old. Away from home. A new environment.

The three-sport star from Lincoln High School wouldn't be the big star here. This was college. The players would be bigger and better. He didn't even know how much he would play. In '54 freshmen didn't play varsity ball. It would be 18 more years before freshmen would be eligible. Also, it was the era of the two-way football player. Nehlen still had only about 140 pounds on his 5-11 frame. Sixty-minute players usually came in larger packages.

He enrolled in classes geared for accounting. At that time, he thought about following in his dad's footsteps. Being a football coach was the farthest thing from his mind. He still had a dream of becoming a major league baseball player. Football was still just a sport to pass the time until another baseball season rolled around. Also, it kept him in contact with two of his former Lincoln High School teammates — little running back Vic DeOrio and guard Larry Kelly, who got scholarships to Bowling Green, too, and were to become his roommates.

Bowling Green football wasn't the big sport on campus. Not then. The Falcons, members of the Mid-American Conference, had won just one game the year before and had only one winning season in the last five.

"I remember sitting in the stands with my dad watching the varsity play one Saturday," Nehlen said. "It was homecoming and there were only about 4,000 in the stands. We used to have more than that at our high school games. My dad nudged me with his elbow and said, 'I think you made a good choice of schools, son. You're smart.'

"I said, 'What do you mean?'

"He said, 'This team is bad. If you can't play for this school, you can't play for any school.'

"I pretty much agreed with him. The team only won two games that year."

Unfortunately, it looked as though Nehlen wasn't as smart as he and Dad thought. He didn't do a lot of playing for the freshman football team that season. He was third string. Third-string quarterbacks aren't usually the ones who see action. But he did play enough to earn a frosh letter. He did the same in basketball and baseball to become possibly the last Bowling Green athlete to accomplish that feat.

"Football still wasn't very much in my thinking," he said. "It just wasn't that high on my list of priorities. I guess the truth was I really wasn't sure what I wanted to do. Then along came a man who changed all that and probably has had more influence on my life than anyone I've ever come in contact with."

The man was Doyt Perry, who in the spring of 1955 succeeded Bob Whittaker as head football coach. Perry had been backfield coach on Woody Hayes' staff at Ohio State in 1954 when the Buckeyes won the national championship. Perry changed the fortunes of Bowling Green football and the future of Don Nehlen. Perry hired a disciple of Hayes on his staff, too — Edward (Bo) Schembechler, who was to influence Nehlen 22 years later.

"When Coach Perry came to Bowling Green," Nehlen said, "one of the first things he did was put a notice on the bulletin board in the gym for all quarterback candidates to report to the tennis court. Dale Herbert, the equipment man, announced, 'And the new coach wants all the quarterbacks to wear shorts and T-shirts.'

"Now, I still weighed only about 145 and was still self-conscious about my size. I said, 'Herbie, you got to give me some long sweatpants. I can't go out there with shorts on. Coach will take one look at my skinny legs and either run me off, or laugh his head off.' I didn't think a 145-pound skinny-legged quarterback was what the new coach had in mind.

"Herbie said, 'Coach's orders. Shorts and T-shirt.'

"So, I followed orders and headed for the tennis court. With shorts on there was no way I was going to be able to camouflage my tremendous physique. When I got to the tenins court, Coach Perry was already there with a couple of the other quarterbacks.

"He spotted me walking out and yelled in a menacing voice, 'Hey, you! Off! Get off the court! I'm meeting with my quarterbacks.'

"I said, 'Coach Perry, I am one of your quarterbacks.'

"And I'll bet right then and there he wondered why in the heck he ever left Ohio State to come to Bowling Green. The funny thing was I had been trying like crazy to gain weight ever since I had enrolled at Bowling Green.

"Back then we had to work for our room and board. I had what they called a commodity job. My job was to report to 'The Commons,' where all the students ate, every morning at 5 o'clock and open orange and tomato juice cans. Did that until 7:30. Then I got to eat breakfast. I didn't care for the hours, but it was a good job for someone trying to gain weight."

Teammate Kelly said, "Yeah, Don used to eat two and three breakfasts. It's a good thing he had that job because he sure couldn't have paid for all that food. We used to think he had a tapeworm."

Perry didn't have to wonder about his skinny-legged quarterback very long. When the coach installed his new offense, the split-T formation, Nehlen was made to order for it. In no time at all the third-string freshman quarterback was battling senior Jim Bryan for the starting job.

"As an athlete," Perry said, "Nehlen was head and shoulders above Bryan. He was a pretty good passer and a fine runner. We needed a running quarterback to run the option play. And he was one of the most enthusiastic young men I'd ever seen. He was just go-go all the time."

That enthusiasm was always a big plus for Nehlen. He was constantly trying to do anything to make up for his lack of size. And he was willing to do anything to impress the coach. When you had to go both ways and lacked beef, you weren't exactly the darling of a defensive coach's eyes.

To make matters worse for the little quarterback, Bowling Green, a city of 25,000 located 25 miles south of Toledo, was in the heart of the Ohio flatland. Anyone familiar with flatland knows the wind blows and blows. "It was a tough place to play football," Nehlen said. "Sometimes I felt like asking the coaches to nail my shoes to the ground to keep from blowing away. Throwing the ball in the wind wasn't the easiest thing to do. Punting it was even worse."

And guess who Coach Perry turned into the Falcons' punter?

Nehlen said, "We were scrimmaging one day that spring and coach announced we were going to punt that afternoon. I asked, "Who is the punter, coach?"

"He said, 'You go ahead and punt.'

"I was dumbfounded. I had never punted in my life. I said, 'Me?'

"He said, 'You're a quarterback, aren't you? You're supposed to be an athlete. Punt the ball!'

"I didn't know anything about punting. All I knew was you went back, caught the snap from center and kicked the ball as hard as you could. I didn't even know how to hold it. But I punted that day — and punted for Bowling Green for the next three years. I don't know why he made me the punter. But I can tell you this, when I learned I was, I began to work on it. I said, 'What the heck, if I'm going to punt, I'm not going to go out on the field and embarrass myself.' "

Nehlen didn't set the world on fire as a punter, but he improved enough that in three seasons he averaged 34 yards per kick.

On Sept. 17, 1955, Nehlen, described as a possible "triple-threat," was the starting quarterback for Bowling Green against Defiance College. He completed five of 10 passes for 108 yards and one touchdown as the Falcons romped, 40-0. "I had first-game jitters," he said. "It's a good thing we were playing a team like Defiance and put 40 points on the board. If I'm not mistaken I got so mixed up on one trap play that I handed the ball off to a guard. You might say I was just a little excited."

The following week he started against rival Kent State and suffered what Perry termed, "more sophomore mistakes." The Falcons were tied, 6-6. That was the week Nehlen's employment as a juice-can opener was terminated. He said, "We were supposed to have a team breakfast in The Commons. Coach Perry came through the line and there I was standing there opening cans.

"He said, 'What are you doing?'

"I said, 'This is my job, coach.'

"And he muttered, 'I'm going to change that right now.'

"And I never had to get up at 5 a.m. and open another juice can again."

And it was also the week Nehlen lost his job as No. 1 quarterback. That week Perry decided to go with senior Bryan against conference foe Western Michigan. Nehlen, although relegated to No. 2 quarterback, still punted and returned kickoffs. With vet Bryan, according to Perry "a better passer," at the controls, the Falcons blanked Western Michigan, 35-0.

Nehlen played in a reserve role until the eighth game of the season. The opponent that week was arch-rival Miami of Ohio, undefeated and ranked 10th in the nation. Bowling Green came into the game with a 6-0-1 record, but minus veteran Bryan. He had been hospitalized with an injured knee two days before the game. Headlines in the Bowling Green *Sentinel-Tribune* read, "Soph QB Nehlen Back At The Helm."

The Falcons didn't win the game. In fact, Nehlen bobbled a snap from center on a punt that resulted in Miami eking out a 7-0 victory. But something else happened that afternoon. It was the day Don Nehlen became the No. 1 quarterback for good and the undisputed leader of the Falcons. Teammate Kelly said, "Don took the team right down the field, mostly on runs off the option play. We didn't score, but from that day on he was the leader of our football team. His enthusiasm became contagious. He led by example. I mean, here was this skinny sophomore now the recognized leader of the team."

Perry said, "I know that Don became the leader of the team, but I don't remember when it happened. The players would know more about that. To be a leader you have to be confident of your own ability. You don't just go out on the field and yell, whoop and holler. Don didn't have much size then. And today he wouldn't be high on anybody's recruiting list. But he had the intangibles and the confidence."

"I remember dropping that snap in the Miami game," Nehlen said. "I think I recovered it. But it was fourth down, so it didn't matter much.

When Miami got down near our goal, the free safety, which was me, had to move up the line of scrimmage and play middle linebacker. Here I was at 145 pounds playing middle linebacker on the goal line against the 10th-rated team in America. Now that I think about it, it was laughable. Miami just handed the ball to their big fullback and he went 'Pffft!' and just ran right over me. So, I not only gave them the ball, they ran right over the top of me to score.''

The final game of the season was in Athens against Ohio University, a team the Falcons hadn't beaten in seven years. Nehlen threw for the only scores in a 13-0 victory and Bowling Green ended with a 7-1-1 record, a second-place finish in the conference and its best record since 1948.

Along about this time Nehlen's thinking toward football began to change, and his interest in baseball and basketball diminished. "When I saw Coach Perry's approach to coaching," he said, "I decided that was what I wanted to do."

Thoughts of being an accountant like his dad vanished. He switched his major to education. The dream of being a major league baseball player was put on the back burner, too, although he would still play for the Falcons each spring and became their captain his junior year.

"Suddenly, football became fun," Nehlen said. "Oh, sure, it was all business. But there was a plan. Coach Perry put all the gears in motion. Before him Bowling Green had been a loser. In one year he turned the program into a winner. It was the same school. The same players. But now we were winning.

"I'd go by the coaches' offices late at night and the lights would be on. I wanted to be part of that. I liked the way the coaches took a personal interest in us. They'd come by the dorms and see us. The entire concept of football took on a new meaning for me.

"I had Coach Perry for class and used to go to his office and talk to him about coach-player relationships, coach-coach relationships, how to teach this, how to teach that, how to handle people. I admired him so much. And somewhere along the way I decided I wanted to be a football coach. His approach was just different than anything I had been exposed to before.

"I never wanted to be like him. That would have been silly. But a lot of the things he taught me in those early days are foundations I still use — and are things Bo Schembechler (now the legendary coach at Michigan) still uses."

Perry influenced many young men in the 10 years he coached the Falcons. When he quit coaching in 1966 to become the Falcons' athletic director, he had compiled a 77-11-5 record, won six Mid-American Conference championships, won the NCAA Division II national title in 1959 and is one of the few living coaches to ever have a stadium named after him. Also, in the 1960s Bowling Green was second only to Alabama as the nation's winningest team.

"Perry said, "Everybody makes so much of my coaching record at Bowling Green, but I couldn't have done it if I hadn't had boys like Don Nehlen. He was a heck of an athlete. What he lacked in size he made up for with intelligence and enthusiasm. He was a student of the

game, was like a coach on the field and was the darnedest worker you ever saw. And he called all his own plays. The game was a little different then. He was one of the ones who got my program off to a great start. Check the record. Don Nehlen played in only two losing football games in three years here. Now, if you lose only two games in three years, that means one was an undefeated season."

That one came in 1956, Nehlen's junior year. It began with a bang.

It was a windy, rainy Sept. 15 afternoon in Bowling Green's old University Stadium and Nehlen got the season off to a rousing beginning by quarterbacking the Falcons to a 73-0 rout of Defiance. It was the most points ever scored by a Bowling Green team. And in the ensuing weeks the Falcons blanked Kent State, 17-0; beat Western Michigan, 27-13; trounced Drake, 46-7; beat Baldwin-Wallace, 34-21, thanks to Nehlen's 69-yard touchdown run and 105 yards rushing on five carries; beat Toledo, 34-12, with Nehlen making a key interception to save a first-half touchdown; and beat Marshall, 34-12, before a then record home crowd of 7,700; and tied Miami, 7-7, which at the time was again in the top 20. Nehlen came up with another key interception in this game.

Bowling Green sportswriter Dean Roach wrote, "Nehlen's defensive ability cannot compare to his running ability. His forte is, and always has been, the option play. He picked up sizeable chunks of yardage against Miami with his swivel-hipped runs. Several times when trapped he twisted, rolled off and spun away from tacklers."

"As I remember," Nehlen said, "Miami tied us. We didn't tie them."

And on Nov. 10, Nehlen clinched the first conference championship for Perry as he completed eight of 15 passes for 151 yards and scored on a nine-yard run in a 41-27 win over Ohio University. Bowling Green ended the season, 8-0-1, for only its fourth unbeaten season in 38 years of football.

The beginning of his senior season at Bowling Green was almost a carbon copy of the previous one as he sparked the Falcons past Baldwin-Wallace, 60-7. Following that was a 16-0 blanking of Xavier.

Then came one of the games Nehlen remembers best. "It was on Oct. 5, 1957," he said. "We were playing at Delaware. Delaware was a small school and wasn't exactly a big game for us. But it did have great tradition. We came in unbeaten (3-0) and hadn't lost a game since that 7-0 loss at Miami in 1955. Maybe we were a little overconfident. I don't know. But I do know we had one of those games where we couldn't do anything right.

"Now, you have to understand, Coach Perry was from the old school. We didn't do a lot of fancy stuff. That meant our passing attack was very limited. In two previous seasons as quarterback I had thrown only 93 passes. Never threw more than eight, 10, 12 passes a game. We had one pass play where both tight ends hooked and one where the halfback would run to the flat and then go down the sideline. It was called a 'deep left, or deep right,' depending on which way we ran it. That was it.

"In those days, our formation was two tight ends and

three running backs. No wide receivers. No crossing patterns. No delays. No bootlegs. Most of the time we just got the ball, lined up and 'pow!'

"It was late in the fourth quarter with the score 0-0. We had possession on our own 33. It was third down and 31 yards to go for a first down. I called the halfback pass. Don't remember whether I called it left, or right. The halfback was a guy named Bob Ramlow.

"I took the snap, faded back to about my 20 and hit Ramlow for a 67-yard touchdown pass play and we won, 7-0.

"It's odd that I don't remember the scores of most games. That's too many games ago. But I remember certain plays. That one I remember because it was a third-and-31 and turned out to be a game-winner. I laugh every time I think about it, because it was an illegal play. We had an ineligible man downfield. Our right guard was so far into the secondary I think the officials thought he was a receiver. That has to be the only reason they didn't call the play back."

Nehlen wasn't always making like a junior Jack Armstrong. The week after the heroics at Delaware, the Falcons were tied by Western Michigan, 14-14. And it was a pass interception thrown by Nehlen with seven minutes to play that resulted in the Broncos' tying touchdown. "The quarterback who never threw an interception is like the runner who never fumbled," said Nehlen with a smile. "He never played."

The next week Nehlen was back to his old tricks. He completed six of six passes for 110 yards and two touchdowns and scored once himself on a twisting 19-yard run to lead Bowling Green past Toledo, 29-0. The next game he engineered a 68-yard drive late in the fourth quarter as the Falcons edged Kent State, 13-7. Also, he intercepted a pass on his own two-yard line in the closing seconds of the first half to thwart a Kent State scoring threat.

The following week, Nov. 2, Bowling Green entertained rival Miami again. The Falcons were unbeaten. So were the Redskins — as usual. It was another record University Stadium crowd — and another cold, windy day in the Ohio flatland south of Lake Erie.

It was in the second half with the score tied, 7-7. Nehlen had completed 10 of 12 passes for 110 yards. Fans were cheering, hoping he could pull another trick out of the bag. But it wasn't to be.

Miami had the ball and a Redskins' runner broke through a gaping hole in the line. Nehlen came up from his safety position to make the tackle. He put his weight into the runner (by now he weighed 185 pounds) and the runner put his weight into breaking the tackle. Nehlen made the tackle. But when he made the hit, the protective face bar on his helmet — players wore only one bar back in the 1950s — snapped and pierced the corner of his left eye.

He was carried off the field and Bowling Green went on to lose, 13-7.

"I thought sure I was going to lose the eye, or at least lose my sight in that eye," he said. "It was bad and looked terrible. After about four days, though, the swelling

started going down and darned if I couldn't see out of it. I guess the good lord was with me. Outside of the broken collarbone my sophomore year in high school, this was the only other injury I'd ever had. But I thought this one was going to be serious."

Once he learned his sight was okay, there was no way he was going to stay on the sidelines. He returned to practice and played the following week in a 7-7 tie with Ohio University.

On Nov. 16 he ended his playing career at Fairfield Stadium in Huntington, W.Va., against Marshall University (then Marshall College). He threw a nine-yard touchdown pass to teammate DeOrio. And late in the game, he intercepted a pass deep in Bowling Green territory to preserve a 14-7 win.

"Even though we had great teams at Bowling Green, Marshall was always a thorn in our side," he said. "They never won very many games, but for some reason always gave us fits. About the only thing I remember about that game was it was played in ankle-deep mud."

In three seasons he played in two losing football games (those 7-0 and 13-7) losses to Miami). Bowling Green compiled records of 7-1-1, 8-0-1, and 6-1-2 and scored 702 points to 207 for the opposition.

On a team that didn't throw much, he completed 80 of 153 passes (52.3 percent) for 1,173 yards and 10 touchdowns. He threw 13 interceptions. He gained 271 yards rushing and scored six touchdowns. He averaged 16.5 yards on kickoff returns, punted for a 34-yard average and on defense intercepted six passes and returned them for a 17.5-yard average. And he was named the second team All-Mid-American Conference quarterback his junior and senior years.

Now that his football days were over, Nehlen once again turned his attention to baseball and tried to play third base one last time for the Falcons. After 15 games he discovered baseball wasn't his first love anymore. Football was.

Tom Kisselle, who was a senior on the Bowling Green team when Nehlen was a sophomore, knew from the start the skinny kid with the crewcut would be a football coach. Kisselle would later coach under Nehlen, serve as the Falcons' assistant athletic director and become one of Nehlen's best friends.

He said, "The thing that always stood out about Don was that he was always so enthusiastic about everything he did. And when he got interested in football, he ate and slept it. I don't think any of us lived with the game all the time like he did. And some of us were pretty gung-ho about it.

"My last year in school there was a group of us who wanted to coach. There was me, Don, Jack Hecker (now Kisselle's brother-in-law and on the Army coaching staff), Bill Lyons (who coached for a while in the Toledo school system) and a couple of other guys.

"We put together the darnedest football notebook you ever saw. We spent our time picking the brains of our coaches and putting their ideas, plus some additions of our own, in a notebook. We thought we had a unique oppor-

11

tunity since we were around great coaches like Perry and Schembechler. And Don was the most enthusiastic. He drew X's and O's all the time. He'd do it in his room. If he happened to be out cruising in that 'Brown Bomber' and spotted a light on in the football office as he passed, he'd stop and go in and talk football with whoever happened to be there."

Jack Harbaugh, former Falcon and now head coach at Western Michigan, recalls his first remembrances of Nehlen. Harbaugh, who would later coach under Nehlen, too, said, "It was in 1957. I had just met him. He was a senior, the leader of the team. I was just a freshman. I figured the senior quarterback would be a guy who knew it all — or thought he did.

"The thing that impressed me about him was he was obsessed with being successful. And he tried to leave no stone unturned. I remember right after I met him, I went into his room one night and there he was looking at the football rulebook.

"I asked, 'What are you doing?'

"He answered, 'Memorizing the book.'

"I exclaimed, ''All of it!'

"And he said, 'Yes. And I'm underlining the rules that affect the play of the quarterback.'

"The guy was and is a student of the game."

Don Nehlen, age 22, couldn't wait for his chance to show off what he had learned. It would come sooner than he expected.

Chapter Four

Two important events occurred in Nehlen's life during the summer of 1958: he married Merry Ann Chopson, and he got his first coaching job.

"It seems like Merry Ann and I had known each other forever," he said. "We went to school from the third grade on. We had gone steady since my junior year in high school and had been engaged since my junior year in college. Besides, I figured we had been apart long enough."

Merry Ann didn't go to college. Her family didn't have the money. In fact, Merry Ann and Don paid for their own wedding when they were married on July 26. They had what is called a "Bridal Dance" at a dance hall. Friends threw money in an old galvanized wash bucket for the privilege of dancing with Merry Ann. Afterward, Merry Ann and Don sat down, counted the money and found they had $400, more than enough to finance a three-day honeymoon to Niagara Falls. Times were tough.

Nehlen's first job came as a result of his mentor, Bowling Green Coach Doyt Perry. "I told Coach Perry I wanted to go into coaching," Nehlen said. "This was back in May when I had given up playing baseball for the university team and was student teaching. He told me about an assistant's job at Mansfield, Ohio, Senior High School and set up an interview for me.

"I drove to Mansfield, met the coach, Tom Pierson, and the principal and two weeks later got the job. It was coaching sophomore football, basketball and baseball. It wasn't a great job and the money wasn't much, either. I made $3,200 a year for coaching three sports and teaching geography, health and physical education. But I was only 22 and it was a start in coaching."

Forunately, the newlyweds didn't have to live on that $3,200 long. After Nehlen had been on the job for one football season, old friend Earl Schreiber from Canton drove over to Mansfield and took Don and Merry Ann out to dinner.

"We were sitting at the dinner table," Nehlen said, "and Earl asked, 'Bonesey, what do you want to do?' He always called me that. Still does today.

"I said, 'Earl, I think I'm a football coach, but I don't know. I'd like to find out, especially find out if I'm a head coach.'

"He said, 'If that's what you want, I'll see what I can do.'

"And about four months later I got a call from Harold Walker, then the head of Canton Local School District, about the head coaching position at Canton South High School."

Schreiber expained why he asked Nehlen "what he wanted to do?" that night in Mansfield. "I thought perhaps we could still get Bonesey to go to work for Timken," he said. "He had worked for us every summer since he was 16. We had many fine young men work in our recreation program — guys like George Saimes (Michigan State All-American running back and now scout for the Tampa Bay Buccaneers of the National Football League), Vince Costello (former Cleveland Browns linebacker), Don James (now head football coach at the University of Washington), Jim Swierczek (former great Marshall University end).

"Bonesey was the best of the lot. We organized the first Little League baseball teams in Canton. He was very instrumental in that. We developed a fitness program for youngsters in our day camps. He was right in the middle of that, too. He seemed to have a knack for getting youngsters to do things.

"You know, when you try to keep 80 or 100 little people occupied all day, there are always a few who are difficult to handle. Bonesey never had any trouble.

"I remember one day he took a bunch of kids who seemed to do nothing but get into trouble. He took these troublemakers off to the side and devised a game for them to play. It wasn't anything fancy. All he did was put a little rock on top of a big rock and had the youngsters throw pebbles and try to knock the little one off the big one.

"He kept those kids busy all afternoon. Now, we had a lot of supervisors on our summer staff who had all kinds of degrees in psychology and recreation. I called their attention to what Bonesey was doing with those kids. I said, 'You people have all those degrees, and yet you couldn't do a thing with those troublemakers. That guy found something for them to do — something that was fun. They didn't teach you that in college, did they?'

"It gave me an indication that Don Nehlen had leadership qualities. If he hadn't been bent on being a coach, I'm sure he would have been a fine employee for our company."

Schreiber admits he "might have had something to do" with Nehlen getting the call about the Canton South job. But Nehlen was just one of 30 candidates being interviewed. Besides, it wasn't the greatest of jobs. Canton South hadn't had a winning football team in eight years. That year it was barely over .500 (4-3-1). In 1958 the team under coach Cy Lane was 0-9.

The football field the team played on wasn't exactly what you would call a stadium. It had no fence around it.

The stands were small. And there was a creek running just back of one end zone. Every extra point kicked that way went into the creek. Most fans who attended the games didn't pay. They simply walked in.

Also, at that time, South, under veteran basketball coach Red Ash, was a basketball power. Ash was one of the most successful high school coaches in the state.

Nehlen said, "All the coaches who had applied for the job were well-dressed when they went in for their interviews. A lot of them carried movie projectors to show the screening committee their teams in action. Me? I was wearing the one sport coat and one good pair of trousers I owned. And I had no projector. Even if I'd had one, I didn't have any films of my teams in action. You didn't film sophomore high school teams."

What Nehlen had was what he had always had — unbounded enthusiasm and supreme confidence in himself. And that's what he offered the committee.

He went into the interview room and said, "I don't have a projector or any film. I don't even own a suit. All I have to my name is a lot of enthusiasm. This school has had eight straight losing seasons and didn't win a single game last year. You don't need any experienced coaches coming here to retire.

"What you need is some guy who is ready to come here and turn things around."

Larry Kelly, his former Bowling Green teammate, said, "Don was positive in that interview. But the committee couldn't make up its mind and it kept calling him back again and again as it gradually eliminated candidates. He finally told them that if they didn't decide on a choice pretty soon, he wouldn't be able to afford to keep driving the 75 miles from Mansfield to Canton. The committee ended up paying him mileage. Can you believe that? They didn't pay mileage in those days for guys who interviewed for high school jobs."

But Nehlen sold himself. And in April 1959, Don Nehlen, age 23 years, three months and 19 days, was named head football coach at Canton South.

Walker, the head of the school district, said, "We are happy to get someone the caliber of Don Nehlen. We hope we can become better organized and ultimately produce a winning football team."

"I was thrilled about getting the job for several reasons," Nehlen said. "The job was just outside Canton and that meant I was going home. Also, I could still have my summer job for the Timken Company. You have to understand my salary at South was $4,025, but I could earn another $1,000 in the summer. Without that summer job, Merry Ann and I would have been hard-pressed to make it."

Coaching football was just part of Nehlen's job. The rest involved being an "itinerant teacher" in the grade schools (grades one through eight) in the Canton South School District.

Nehlen traveled around each day to Trump Road, North Industry, Prairie College and Amos McDaniel schools and taught physical education. "I'd put one of those small, round trampolines in the back of my old Plymouth (the "Brown Bomber" his dad had given him when he went off to college was long gone) and off I'd go on my rounds of the schools," he said. "It was the most fun I ever had. I was surprised how much I enjoyed teaching boys and girls that age. I loved it — and them."

Nehlen may have been one of the first coaches in America to let a girl play football with the boys. His sister Carolyn said, "This little girl always hung around when Donnie organized the boys in touch football games. She wanted to play. Donnie let her. He was probably the only coach who would have done that. And today this girl, now a young woman, thinks Donnie is the greatest. By the way, so do I."

The breaking of the rules resulted because he was gung-ho and because of his summer employment at Timken. Prior to the start of that first season, Nehlen was assigned to a strange job by the company. He was actually paid to "guard the lake" at Timken Park. "I know that sounds funny," he said. "But there was a big lake in the park and part of my job was to guard it and make sure no one fell in and drowned — or got hurt. The company didn't want any lawsuits. My dad always kidded me about that job.

"He'd say, 'You gotta guard the pond? Why? Is somebody going to steal it?' He always thought that was funny — guarding a lake!"

On Sunday mornings when Nehlen was "on guard," he was doing something else, too. A few of his South football players always happened to drop by, and their new head coach would take them behind the trees by the lake and managed to put in a few offensive plays and defensive alignments. "Sure, it was illegal," he said. "You weren't allowed to do that. But I was young, full of vinegar and couldn't wait to get started.

"Now, I didn't have my entire team over there behind those trees. It wasn't a full-fledged practice. Just a few players who 'happened' to drop by on Sunday mornings. I figured, 'Hey, we might as well be doing something.' The South football program was so bad. I was just trying to create some enthusiasm among my players."

Nehlen created something else, too — a new look around the school. He and Larry Kelly, whom he had hired as one of his assistants, would go to the school on Saturday nights and work cleaning and painting the locker room. That almost got Nehlen in trouble because one night about 11 o'clock he was on top of the lockers scrubbing them and Kelly was washing down the floor with a hose and in walked a school board member. He was driving by and saw the lights on and thought someone was breaking into the school.

He said, "Coach, what in the heck are you doing?"

Nehlen said, "I'm cleaning up this place. It's filthy."

The young coach didn't get into trouble with the school board member, but when word got back to the school janitors about the "filthy" locker room, it did make them all mad at him. "I kinda sensed they didn't like me," Nehlen said. "Here I was a young whippersnapper coming in and badmouthing their work right off the bat. But I had always prided myself on being able to get along with people, and before long I had them on my side and they cleaned the heck out of the locker room after that.

"We did more than just clean and paint the locker room. We had to line the practice field. We made our own weights. We did everything you could imagine. South didn't have any money, but it was a good school."

Nehlen's first game as a head football coach laid the cornerstone for a nickname he would later acquire — "Master of Upsets."

It was on Sept. 18, 1959. The new coach took his tiny Canton South Wildcat team, a team which was 0-9 the season before, to Massillon to play Massillon Jackson High School, the defending league champions. Suffice to say, Nehlen's team was a heavy underdog.

"We had the littlest football team you ever saw," he said. "My guards, tackles and center were tiny. None weighed more than 150 pounds. But they were like their coach. They had a lot of fight in them. Massillon Jackson was 'THE' team in our league and coached by a man named Bob Fife, a guy who worked with me in the summers at Timken."

Final score was: Canton South 14, Massillon Jackson 7.

"I'll never forget that game as long as I live," said Nehlen. "It was the school's first victory since the 1957 season. My players carried me off the field — and darned near killed me. When we got into the locker room, there all of my players sat on the floor, put their heads down and cried like babies. I cried with them. Most of these kids had never played in a winning football game. It was my first win as a head coach — my first win as a head coach of a high school in my hometown. It was quite an emotional experience.

"Now, it doesn't rank up there with a West Virginia University win over Pitt. But at that time in my career it was a heck of a win."

A local sportswriter wrote, "You think the Russians rejoiced when they hit the moon with a rocket? That celebration was nothing compared to the one Canton South Wildcat fans uncorked last night. It was quite a coaching debut for the former Lincoln High School and Bowling Green University gridiron ace."

Jackson Coach Fife said, "Don Nehlen simply had his team ready to play enthusiastic football. His kids wanted it more. Don did an amazing job in such a short time of getting them ready to play."

The following week Nehlen and his Wildcats got victory No. 2, a 20-0 shutout over Perry High School. Quarterback Tim Miller, whose younger brother, Mark, would later play for Nehlen in college, threw three touchdown passes. It was the first time a South team had won its first two games since 1948.

Headlines the next week were: "Upstart Canton South battles favored Glenwood to a 0-0 deadlock before 4,000 screaming fans. Coach Don Nehlen's Wildcats stop Glenwood twice inside the two-yard line in the last 90 seconds of the game. It was a cardiac special all the way."

In the following Monday's Associated Press high school poll, which was the "official" poll in Ohio, Canton South actually received a few votes in the poll. That was a first. South fans were delirious.

A third victory came the next week, 26-0, over Sandy Valley. Believe it or not, Nehlen's Wildcats were unbeaten (3-0-1). At this point the miracle ended. Nehlen suffered his first defeat as a coach on Oct. 16, 1959, in a 8-0 loss to Lehman High School.

But that first team wasn't a loser. It finished the '59 season with a 4-4-1 record. At the post-season football banquet, you would have thought Nehlen and his team had won the county championship. "The boosters gave me a topcoat and a new camera," Nehlen said. "It was unbelievable. And it was probably the most rewarding year I've ever had as a coach."

Nehlen's second team at Canton South was 5-4 and gave him his first winning season. And then came his third year with the Wildcats — 1961. Nehlen's team finished with a 6-2-1 record and tied Perry High School for the Stark County championship. One of Nehlen's assistant coaches that year was Ron Blackledge, now an assistant coach for the Pittsburgh Steelers and father of former Penn State quarterback Todd Blackledge.

Dick White, who used to stay at the Nehlen house and shoot marbles with little Donnie years ago, said, "In three years he turned Canton South from a basketball school to a football school."

Nehlen laughed and said, "I don't know if I did that, but we sure made a dent in it." And along about this time Nehlen began speaking to Parent Teacher Association meetings all over the district stressing the need for a new football stadium.

The 1962 season was Nehlen's fourth, last and best at South. His Wildcats finished 9-1, won the county title and finished second in the Ohio Class AA AP poll. At the beginning of the year, Nehlen said, "We started three years ago and now I think we have the finest team in Stark County."

There were a few dissenters. "The big tough Wildcats are favored to win the county Class AA league this year," wrote the local writers. "If there were any doubters in the strength of the Canton South football team, they have suddenly become believers."

South won its first game over Lincoln, Nehlen's old high school, 32-12 — the Wildcats first win ever over Lincoln. Hopes for an undefeated season were smashed the next week when Louisville won in an upset, 14-6. And then Nehlen's team went on a rampage and won eight straight games by scores of 40-0, 12-6, 50-6, 36-6, 46-0, 37-8, 53-0 and 64-0. It scored a school record 376 points and held opponents to only 52.

Nehlen commented, "It was a great year, but we should have won the one we lost." It's worth noting that the next year South got its new stadium.

When the '62 season was over, one of Nehlen's players, a guard named Larry Cox, was being recruited by University of Cincinnati Coach Chuck Studley, now the defensive coordinator for the Miami Dolphins. Nehlen drove the players down for a recruiting visit. The direct result of the visit was that shortly after that, Nehlen was

15

offered and accepted his first job on a college staff.

Nehlen said, "I didn't apply for the job. And I never quite figured out whether Studley offered me the job as his backfield coach because of my coaching ability, or because I was a good handball player." And Nehlen was a good one. Four years earlier he won the Mansfield city championship and before that he was considered the best handball player on the Bowling Green campus. There were some who felt he could have been a nationally ranked player if he had really worked at it.

"While we were in Cincinnati," Nehlen said, explaining about the handball bit, "Coach Studley was moaning over the fact that he had no one to play handball with. He said, 'I sure would like to play a few games of handball to relax. I need to unwind.'

"I said, 'I'd like to play some handball, too.'

"And he asked, 'Do you play handball?'

" 'Yes, but I don't have any gear,' I said. Several of his assistant coaches tried to warn me not to get on the court with him. 'He's too good for you — one of the best in Cincinnati,' they said. Well, I was pretty good myself. Anyhow, he rounded up some gear for me and we went at it. Played three games and all three were 21-20. He won two and I won one.

"As soon as he got an opening on his staff he called me. I said, 'Do you want a coach or a handball player.' He said, 'I might as well get 'em both while I'm at it.' I'll tell you this — we used to have some hard-fought games. We'd tangle almost every day at noon. It got to the point that when the players heard we were going at it, most would come over to watch.

"I attended a clinic in Washington, D.C., after I left Studley's staff. He was coming in for the same clinic. He called me from Cincinnati and told me to meet him at the airport and to bring my handball gear. I said, 'Why?'

"He said, 'I know a couple of generals at the Pentagon and we're going to play handball at the Pentagon.'

"We did, too. Must have played for five hours. My hands were so sore after that, I couldn't walk."

Nehlen stayed on the Cincinnati staff just for the 1963 season. The Bearcats were 6-4. In the spring of 1964 he was offered the job as head coach at "THE" high school in his hometown — Canton McKinley. That same spring a man named Earle Bruce (now head coach at Ohio State) was named coach at nearby Massillon. Nehlen and Bruce were to have a memorable encounter.

"At that time, the Canton McKinley job was probably the second-best high school coaching position in the country," Nehlen said. "Massillon was the best. Besides, it meant I was going back home again. They offered me $10,000 a year and gave me a car to drive."

He couldn't refuse the offer.

McKinley played its games in 12,000-seat Fawcett Stadium, the stadium where the annual Pro Football Hall of Fame game is played every July. As a boy Nehlen used to sneak into the stadium to watch McKinley play. He wouldn't have to sneak in anymore, because now he was going to be the coach.

Finally, he was going to make a decent salary. He and

Merry Ann, now the parents of two children — Danny, born April 21, 1960, and Vicki, born Feb. 24, 1962, would actually have enough extra money to go to a movie once in a while. They would have their first real home. Not an apartment.

Nehlen, who had left Canton South the year before coaching a team that scored 376 points and compiled a 9-1 record, had a tough act to follow — his own.

That season at McKinley he tried something new, too. Nehlen began to work on his theory of motivating players with certain subtle tricks. One of these was to award his players T-shirts with slogans on them and have them wear them under their uniforms. A little thing, but little things often are what motivate. Nehlen was beginning to learn that a large part of playing football was between the ears.

Mike Norchia, one of his assistant coaches, said, "Don was great for working on the kids' heads as much as their physical talent. That was back when the mental part of the game wasn't stressed as much as it is now. He had the players wearing T-shirts with words on them like 'hustle' and 'fight' and 'spirit.' And he was so vibrant, always hustling. It carried over to his players. He just had a knack for taking a mediocre team and making a winner out of it.

"His hustle was contagious. All of his assistants did the same — because of him. And he didn't smoke or drink. Never has. I used to have a party every year and invite all the coaches over to my house to watch the New Year's Day bowl games. I'd have maybe four or five bottles of whiskey, three or four cases of beer and a case of soda pop.

"Well, when I was on Don's staff I always had to send out and buy another couple cases of pop. He didn't drink alcohol and none of the rest of the guys would, either.

"Yeah, I know, he sounds too good to be true. But that was Don. He practiced what he preached. Always did."

Nehlen's McKinley Bulldogs that year may have been his best high school team ever. It won nine consecutive games; romped over four opponents by scores of 50-0, 53-0, 62-0 and 70-0; played before home crowds of 10,000 to 13,000; and was ranked No. 2 in the Ohio AP poll.

The team ranked No. 1 was Bruce's Massillon Tigers, also 9-0. And the last game looming on McKinley's schedule was — MASSILLON in Massillon's Tiger Stadium for the Class A (big school) championship of Ohio. The 69th meeting between the two high school powerhouses in a series that began in 1894.

Pre-game buildup was tremendous. McKinley, with a high-scoring attack, had scored 365 points and limited opponents to only 40. Massillon had scored 227 to its foes' 34. "A test of McKinley's power vs. Massillon's speed and agility," wrote one sportswriter. The game was to be televised live in Cleveland. ABC-TV sent a crew to Massillon to film the pre-game hoopla for a special it was doing on high school football. Rabid fans from both cities bet enormous sums of money on the game.

And on a sunny Nov. 14 afternoon in front of a standing-room-only crowd of 22,685, McKinley and

Massilon clashed for the mythical state crown.

McKinley, led by quarterback Larry Haines, led 14-0 into the third quarter. Then tragedy struck. Haines was injured and had to leave the game. Nehlen was minus his veteran quarterback. Massillon rallied and scored three times thanks to its speed, and, according to Nehlen, "a few breaks from the officials." The Tiger's winning touchdown came with 54 seconds to play.

And when the final gun went off, McKinley was on the Massillon 17-yard line — and out of time. It was a heartbreaking defeat for Nehlen and his team. "We just ran out of time," he said.

It was another 9-1 record. Nehlen's second in a row as a high school coach. His last two teams scored an astounding 775 points (38.7 per game), gave up 112 (5.6) and finished second in the final high school polls.

After the season was over, Nehlen received a call from Woody Hayes at Ohio State and was asked if he'd be interested in coming down to Columbus for an interview. Nehlen did and was offered a job on Hayes' staff.

"I was very close to taking the job," Nehlen said. "But something in the back of my mind whispered, 'No, don't take it.' So, I turned it down. Don't ask me why. I don't know. I just knew I had one of the best high school jobs in the country. I had 14 assistants. Yes, fourteen. I had an equipment man. We averaged about 12,000 at home games. I had a $100,000 a year budget. I made $10,000 a year, which was pretty good money in those days. We had a house. We had a car.

"It was the first job I'd had that was solid. Merry Ann and I even had a few dollars in the bank, not much, but a few. And you have to remember, I had been at Mansfield, Canton South, Cincinnati and back to Canton McKinley in the space of six years. That would mean another move.

"Something just told me not to take Coach Hayes' offer. My dad thought I was crazy. So did a lot of my coaching friends."

It was another job that came Nehlen's way. Another job he had not applied for. And a few weeks after that, the phone rang in his McKinley High School office. It was a man named Bob Gibson, head coach at Bowling Green, Nehlen's alma mater. Gibson offered me a job as end coach. Gibson replaced Doyt Perry, who resigned as coach to devote full time to being athletic director.

Nehlen turned Gibson's offer down. He said, "I told Gibby I had aspirations of being a college coach. But the next time I went into college coaching I wanted to go as a coordinator. And I told him, 'Besides, I'm happy here at McKinley.;

"Well, a few weeks after that, Gibby called back and offered me the position as his defensive coordinator. I talked it over with Merry Ann and she didn't want to move. She hadn't gone to school in Bowling Green and really didn't like the place, or thought she didn't. She didn't know anything about Bowling Green.

"But Coach Perry talked to me and said I was one of his most successful graduates. And if Gibson should leave Bowling Green, I would at least be given an interview for the head coaching job. No guarantee, but . . .

"I thought it was worth the chance and I accepted Gibby's offer. We were moving again, back to my alma mater."

Chapter Five

Junior quarterback Russ Jacques was asleep in his bed in his Bowling Green State University dormitory room. Sunlight was filtering around the edges of the window curtains. It was dawn and promised to be another hot, steaming middle-of-August day.

It was two-a-day practice time for the Falcons, and Jacques didn't particularly want to crawl out of bed. His muscles and bones ached. They always did during two-a-days. But he was lying there waiting for the door to open and for "it" to happen.

And it did, just as it did every morning at dawn.

Suddenly, the door was thrust open and a young, enthusiastic guy with a crewcut stuck his head in and yelled, "Everybody up!"

"The sun is shining and the Lord is up there saying, 'STICK 'EM!' Let's go. Up and at 'em!"

That was Jacques' earliest recollection of Don Nehlen, newest assistant on head coach Bob Gibson's Bowling Green coaching staff. "He was such a holler-type guy," Jacques said. "He never melted into the background. I can still remember him opening that door and hollering, 'The sun is shining and the Lord is up there . . .' That was his favorite expression."

It was 1965. Nehlen was back at his alma mater and loving it. He had to. Seven months earlier, he had taken a $400 pay cut to leave his head coaching job at Canton McKinley and come to Bowling Green. And he had to leave Merry Ann and the kids back in Canton until he could find a place for them to live. It had been a tough decision. Merry Ann hadn't been happy at the prospect of carting the children across the state of Ohio again.

Thanks to Bowling Green Athletic Director Doyt Perry, his former coach, Nehlen had a free room. That would save some money and enable him to move his family sooner than expected. Now, the room was free, but it might not have been safe.

Nehlen said, "Bowling Green had built a new football stadium out on the edge of town and named it after Coach Perry (Doyt L. Perry Stadium). The team wasn't playing in old University Stadium in the middle of the campus anymore. The old stadium had what was called the 'Stadium Club,' a dormitory, underneath it. I think the dormitory had been condemned. Coach Perry let me and another assistant coach, Tom Kisselle, live there — free. Tom was trying to find a house for him and his wife, too. We were the only ones living in the place.

"Anyhow, we lived there for, oh, I think about three or four months. I do know that Tom moved out before I did."

Nehlen had to live by himself in the condemned dormitory for only about four weeks. Then he found a house to buy. He had a chance to purchase the first home he and Merry Ann had ever owned. But there was one hitch. He had to come up with $1,800 as a down payment. "We managed to come up with the money," Nehlen said, "thanks to my dad, who loaned us $800. That was 1964 and $1,800 was a small fortune then. At least, it was to me."

He bought the home and moved the family to Bowling Green. But when the family came, he had to leave. He spent all of that summer at Kent State, north of Canton, going to summer school to finish work on his master's degree. "It was of the prerequisites for my job at Bowling Green," Nehlen said. "I had to have a master's. I needed one summer to finish, and this was my sixth year of working on it. If I didn't finish it that summer, they were going to start taking credits away from me.

"The tough part was I had just moved the family to Bowling Green from Canton, and now I had to turn around and go back there for the summer.

"Since I hadn't been on the Bowling Green staff but a few months, I wasn't on the college payroll that summer. We made our house payments for June, July and August and had $200 left over. I took $100 and headed for Kent State. Merry Ann kept $100. That's all we had to live off of that summer.

"And you know what? When I got back after summer school, Merry Ann still had $10 of her $100 left. I spent all of mine. We went out to dinner and celebrated me getting my master's. Blew the whole $10."

Nehlen was defensive coordinator for Gibson for three years in which Bowling Green had records of 7-2, 6-3 and 6-4.

Then just before Christmas in 1967, he was in Youngstown, Ohio, on a recruiting trip. He got a phone call from Gibson and the head coach said, "I want you back on campus tomorrow. Something has come up."

Nehlen said, "I thought we had a football player in trouble, or something like that. When I got back to Bowling Green, all the coaches were there. Gibby had called them all in off the road. I thought, 'What the heck is going on?' We were all in the coaches' meeting room staring at each other.

"Gibby came in and started the meeting by saying he didn't think we were going to win because recruiting wasn't going very well. He said he didn't want to be the first loser at Bowling Green. You have to understand, Bowling Green had lost only 20 games in the previous 13 years, had two undefeated seasons and had been national champions once.''

And then Gibson, the man who had been Perry's offensive line coach for nine years and head coach for three, announced, ''I am resigning.'' He was quoted in the December 12 Bowling Green Sentinel-Tribune, ''My reason for resigning is very simple — I no longer want the job.''

Nehlen thought, ''Oh, my gosh. Here I am 31. I just left one of the best high school jobs in America. And now, three years later, I'm unemployed.'' He knew whoever the new coach was, there was no guarantee he would be retained. ''It wasn't a very good feeling,'' he said.

He wasn't sure about his future as an assistant coach at his alma mater, but he was sure of one thing. He was going to apply for job of head coach. It would be the first time he had ever officially applied for any job.

Nehlen applied.

And less than three weeks later, Don Nehlen was named head coach, the 11th one in the 49-year football history of his alma mater. The official announcement was made on Jan. 2, 1968, one day past his 32nd birthday.

Perry said, ''We had about 75 applicants. Every one of the assistant coaches applied for the job. I wasn't on the screening committee, but I was athletic director and Don Nehlen was my choice. Did I have a lot to do with him getting the job? Hey, I was athletic director. I had a heck of a lot to say about who got the job.

''It was my opinion that he was the best man for the job. At the time he was named head coach, he was probably the youngest head coach at a major school in the country — at least, one of the youngest. It was his first college head coaching job. And coaching in college is different from coaching in high school. However, he had been exposed to some good men and good programs. It was a tough decision, but one I would make again if I had to do it all over.''

Nehlen was proud and humble to be only the second former Bowling Green player to be named the Falcons' head coach. The first was Perry.

''From the time I graduated in 1958,'' Nehlen said, ''it was my one desire and ambition to return to Bowling Green as head coach. I didn't think it would come this soon, though. I had set a goal of somewhere around 15 years.''

Nehlen said at the press conference that he hoped to continue the tradition of winning football. ''Bowling Green has always been at the top, or near the top,'' he said. ''Under my leadershp, we expect to stay there.'' Nehlen was asked at the conference how long he had thought about what style of play, what offense and what defense he would use. He answered, ''From the day I graduated.''

The problem was Gibson had known what he was doing. The team Nehlen inherited had only 18 returning Lettermen. And those were from a team that went 6-4 and 2-4 in the Mid-American Conference. The Bowling Green faithful weren't too keen about coaches whose teams finished near the cellar in the conference standings. They were accustomed to what Perry had done with his teams — namely, win six championships and finish second three times in 10 years.

Nehlen began to work. ''I kissed Merry Ann goodbye the day after I got the job and said I'd see her in June,'' he said. ''Our recruiting had slowed. It was becoming more and more difficult to recruit players in Ohio for Bowling Green. I was hoping my connections in and around the Canton area would be helpful. But I had to get on the road and get busy. There was a lot to do. The program had slipped and started to go in the wrong direction. We didn't have many football players.

''I remember Coach Perry saying to me that spring, 'You know what, Don? I don't think you're going to make it with these players. I don't think you're going to win.'

''I disagreed with him. I guess that was my youth talking. I didn't have much experience, but at the time I didn't know it.''

Coaching wasn't all Nehlen had to do. Back in those days at Bowling Green, all coaches had to teach, too. Nehlen was promoted to an assistant professor in health and physical education and taught classes in philosophy of coaching, handball (he was becoming quite skilled in that sport and would later permanently injure his left index finger playing the sport), squash, tennis, softball and ice skating.

''I remember a scrawny little tot hanging around the ice skating rink all the time,'' Nehlen said. ''The kid would try to skate and had to hang onto the railing to keep from falling. His dad was our team photographer.'' That tot was Scotty Hamilton, gold medal winner at the 1984 Olympics in Sarajevo, Yugloslavia.

''Scotty was a little peanut. But look what he accomplished. I turn on the television and he's the best figure skater in the world. Amazing. It just shows you what you can do if you set yourself a goal and work toward it.

Nehlen set himself a goal — of winning the Mid-American Conference championship. Merry Ann and the kids put a sign on the garage of his new home that read, ''Good luck, Coach.'' Some prankster added, ''You'll need it.'' It would prove to be prophetic.

Nehlen's first Bowling Green team was picked to finish last in the conference. But the new coach wasn't about to buy that. He couldn't wait for the '68 season to get under way. Sentinel-Tribune sport editor Dean Roach wrote: ''Don Nehlen is like a little boy getting ready to play with his new birthday gift. I know Don and how much he hates to lose. He even hates to lose to his wife at cards. Unless I miss my guess, there will be lots of excitement this fall.''

On Nehlen's first staff were old friends Tom Kisselle and Jack Harbaugh, Tom Reicosky, Jim Ruehl and Bob Dudley from Gibson's staff and Elliot Uzelac, former Logan, W. Va., High School coach and now assistant coach at Michigan.

His first game was at home against Ball State on Sept. 21, 1968. It was a hot, humid day. The temperature was in the 90s. "We're ready to go," said Nehlen. "There'd better not be anybody in front of our locker room door when we come out on the field. I'm just scared we might get one of our own players hurt coming out of the locker room.

"We're anxious to see if those so-called experts who picked us to finish at the bottom of the conference standings are right. We're going to be a bunch of screaming maniacs this afternoon."

Nehlen promised exciting football, and the fans got it. When the heat wave settled on Doyt L. Perry field that day, the Falcons had rolled up 449 yards total offense and romped to a 62-8 victory. Bowling Green led, 48-0, at halftime. One referee collapsed from the heat and Nehlen suggested that five minutes be cut from the last two quarters, or else his players might "run themselves to death." The Ball State coach agreed.

It was the biggest victory margin since that 73-0 rout of Defiance in 1956 when a player named Don Nehlen quarterbacked the Falcons. That same afternoon a college team in Morgantown, W. Va., struggled past Richmond, 17-0.

"The margin of that first victory was a little surprising," Nehlen said. "I felt we were ready to play. But we didn't have a lot of experience. Why, I had a tackle who weighed only 210 (Carl Battershell, later an assistant under Nehlen). My guards averaged only 205. We weren't exactly your huge college football team."

Bowling Green met what Nehlen called "a huge team" the next week — Dayton. He recited the opponent's weights to newsmen. "I know 'em by heart," he said, "260, 235, 228, 225, 220, 220, 210, 210, 206, 195 and 185. We'll have to throw this week. If we can't, we'll be in trouble."

That week the Falcons' quarterback, P. J. Nyitray, completed 16 of 23 passes for 173 yards, and Bowling Green won again, 20-14. On one play, Nyitray kept the ball on a great fake and scored — and fooled everyone, except one official (who ruled it a TD).

"I stole that play from another high school coach when I was coaching at Canton McKinley," Nehlen said. "In high school that play drove me crazy. We could never figure out who had the ball. So, I figured, 'Why not use it myself?' "

Bowling Green got its third straight win the next game, 17-10, at Western Michigan. It was Nehlen's first conference win. Then came a night game in Toledo's Glass Bowl against the University of Toledo. The teams battled to a 0-0 tie. "I thought I'd find out if we're a great team, or an average one trying to be great," Nehlen said. "But I still don't know. At least, we haven't lost a conference game yet. That's something."

A 30-7 win over Kent State followed, and Bowling Green had a remarkable 4-0-1 record. The Falcons were fourth in the nation in total defense and fourth in scoring defense. But injuries were piling up. Ten players were on the casualty list. And league powerhouse Miami loomed next — at Miami.

On October 26, Nehlen suffered his first defeat as college coach, 31-7. "We couldn't run, couldn't throw and couldn't stop them," he said. "That about sums it up. Maybe we were living on borrowed time."

The Falcons bounced back the next week with a 54-28 Dad's Day romp over Marshall University. Marshall Coach Perry Moss accused Nehlen of "pouring it on" and declined to shake hands with Nehlen after the game. Nehlen said, "What was I supposed to do, tell my players not to try to score? We could have scored at least three more times if I had left my regulars in. I just wanted to make darned sure we didn't lose to a team like Marshall. I thought I was being nice. If I had wanted to run up the score, we wouldn't have scored 54. It would have been 74.

"Moss was a pro. He thought he was going to come in our conference and eat everybody up. He found out we don't play bad football."

That win gave Nehlen's team a 5-1-1 record. The next foe was unbeaten Ohio University (5-0), led by its outstanding quarterback, Cleve Bryant. It was one of those cold, windy days in Bowling Green, but a crowd of 15,223 turned out to see the Falcons lose in a thriller, 28-27, after holding a 27-14 lead going into the fourth quarter. "It's hard for me to believe we lost," he said. "Our kids are really down. Now we have to go on the road for our last two games. Who made up this schedule?"

Nehlen's Falcons lost the next week in the rain and mud at Northern Illinois, 7-6, when the foe returned the opening kickoff 97 yards for a touchdown. The Falcons ended the season with a 44-14 rout of Xavier to finish with a 6-3-1 record, a 3-2-1 conference record and a tie for third place in the standings. Roach wrote: "Nehlen took a team and at one time coached it to a 5-2-1 record with talent many thought wasn't good enough to be 2-6."

Nehlen was runner-up to Ohio U. Coach Bill Hess for 'MAC Coach of the Year.'

His second season as coach of Bowling Green was a disappointing one because his team had a shot at winning the conference championship. The Falcons had just beaten Miami, coached by a guy named Bill Mallory, 3-0. They had 3-1 league record (loss was to Toledo, 27-26) and could conceivably win the crown if they won games over Marshall and Ohio University. Also, that would give Bowling Green a berth in the Tangerine Bowl, which went to the MAC winner.

The Falcons traveled to Huntington, W. Va., and met Marshall on Nov. 1, 1969. The Thundering Herd had the longest non-winning streak in the nation (27 games) and had been put on NCAA probation and indefinitely suspended from the conference for recruiting violations. Rain most of the week had turned the field into a sea of mud.

Marshall held a 21-6 lead in the fourth quarter and won, 21-16, in a stunning upset. Nehlen's Falcons completed 26 of 43 passes for 299 yards — all school records — in an attempt to pull the game out. Nehlen said, "This is the biggest disappointment I've ever had as a head coach. We just lost to a team I considered the poorest on our schedule. We lost five fumbles and threw two interceptions and got behind. When you turn the ball over that many times you don't win. And you can't play catchup in the mud.''

Bowling Green did win at Ohio U. the following week, 23-16, and finish second in the league. And it closed the season with a road loss at West Texas State, 28-12, and a home victory over Northern Illinois, 38-23. Nehlen's second team ended with a 6-4 record.

"It was a frustrating year," he said. "We lost the one-pointer against Toledo in front of the largest crowd to ever see a Bowling Green home game (20,820). We were down 17-0 at the half and came back and had an extra point just die in that daggoned wind.

"And after we got that great win over Miami, we turned around and stunk up the place at Marshall and lost to a team that should never have beaten us. I'll remember that game for a long time."

Nehlen didn't know it, but he had a season coming up that he would remember longer than that.

The 1970 campaign would be Nehlen's worst ever as a head coach and the only losing football team he had ever been associated with, either as a coach or a player (through 1984).

Nehlen would never make excuses for that disastrous season. But that was also the year son Danny, then 10, underwent serious back surgery. It was discovered that he had a missing vertebra. Danny was in a body cast for six weeks, wore a brace for six months and had to learn to walk all over again. "It was a tough time," wife Merry Ann said. "After that surgery, doctors said Danny would never be able to play contact sports. And Danny loved football."

It was a difficult time for the Nehlen family.

Doyt Perry said, "It's a shame what happened to Don's team that year. Everything imaginable that could have happened happened. Injuries. Bad bounces. Mistakes. I felt sorry for Don because I never saw anybody work any harder. He would stay up all night trying to figure out a way to snap the team out of it. Nothing worked. And the funny thing about that year was that Don thought he was going to have one of his best defensive teams ever."

What happened was Bowling Green finished the year with a 2-6-1 record and dead last in the conference. The season started with a 33-14 loss at Utah State. The Falcons blew a 14-12 lead in the fourth quarter. Two of Utah State's scores came on punt returns of 84 and 73 yards. Afterward, Nehlen said, "It's obvious we lack speed."

A 14-14 tie with Dayton in the rain and wind at Bowling Green was followed by another convincing defeat, 23-3, at Western Michigan. "We blundered our way through a frustrating afternoon," moaned Nehlen, as he sat in the locker room with his head in his hands. It was the first time in 17 years a Falcons' team had been winless after three games.

After that, Bowling Green traveled to Toledo and was blanked, 20-0. The Falcons gained just 68 yards rushing and 29 yards passing. Nehlen's team was 0-3-1 and in the league cellar.

One of the two victories came at home the following week over Kent State, 44-0. A 7-3 loss to Miami was next,

followed by the second win, a 26-24 victory over Marshall in which the Falcons had to score 13 points in the fourth quarter to pull it out.

The season ended with consecutive home defeats to Ohio U., 34-7, and West Texas State, 23-7. The final loss came on a cold, snowy day in front of dismal crowd of 6,682. It was Bowling Green's worst record in 16 years and only the eighth time in 52 years of football that the team won two or less games.

Nehlen said, "It's a shame. We worked so hard and have nothing to show for it. We're not that bad a team, but the record says we're terrible."

Phili Villapiano, a linebacker on the team who later became a 13-year pro with the Oakland Raiders and Buffalo Bills, said, "We did have a good defense that year. That was the problem. Because of our enthusiasm we beat ourselves up in practice. The defense literally beat up on the offense. We put three running backs out. Our fullback went out. Maybe we went at it a little too hard. As I remember, every day in practice was like a Super Bowl."

Villapiano, who has played in four Pro Bowls, should know. He wears a Super Bowl ring from Super Bowl XI when the Raiders beat the Minnesota Vikings, 32-14. "I think part of the reason we played poorly was that somehow the word got out he was leaving," Villapiano went on, "and the players felt bad about that. At least, I did."

Nehlen, in an interview after the nightmarish season ended, said, "I don't like to be a loser and I won't be a loser again."

Perry said, "A lot of people think Bowling Green is going down in football. That is a lot of bunk. We have too good a coaching staff for that to happen. Bowling Green will be back, but it will take the darnedest job of coaching ever by the coaches to bring that about."

Nehlen and the Falcons did bounce back in 1971. The team finished 6-4 overall and was second in the conference with a 4-1 record. The Falcons led the league in total offense, averaging 367.4 yards a game. The only league loss was to league champ Toledo, 24-7.

The biggest challenge ever for a Bowling Green football team faced Nehlen's Falcons in 1972. They were to play the most ambitious schedule in school history with the first four games on the road. The early season schedule included Purdue of the Big 10, which was being touted as possible champ of its conference. The Boilermakers were ranked 13th in pre-season polls. After that, the Falcons had to play at conference rival Miami, at Western Mighigan and at defending champ Toledo.

"That's murder," said Nehlen. "Purdue is a powerhouse. But you know, I think our kids can beat them. We'll just have to take our slingshots with us and fire away. My players think they can win, and I'm not going to disagree. My teams have a history of playing well against the big ones. We'll just have to be intelligent and play mistake-free football. One thing we have on our side is that we think we're pretty good, too."

Nehlen was right. Despite being a 20-point underdog and having 31 players miss practice two days before the game because of flu, Nehlen took his Falcons to West Lafayette, Ind., and upset Purdue, 17-14, before a crowd of 51,839 on a 29-yard field goal into the teeth of a 20-mile-an-hour wind by Don Taylor, a freshman kicker from Canton.

It was the first big win over a truly big opponent in Bowling Green history. And Nehlen was named United Press International 'Coach of the Week.' He said, "It's a great honor for me, but my assistant coaches are the ones who did it. Do a story on them. A lot of folks are calling this an upset. I can't really think of it that way because our kids came into this game believing they could win.

"And I told them before the game, 'If we go into the dressing room at halftime down by only one touchdown, we're going to win because we're in better shape.' And we came in at the half and the score was, 14-14. Our kids were jumping up and down."

Gary Tranquill, an assistant coach for Nehlen then and later at West Virginia and now head coach at Navy, said, "I think a lot of folks were learning that Don had a knack for getting his team ready for a big game. He thought his staff was as good as any staff in the country. We felt that way, too."

The following week was arch-rival Miami, and Nehlen had the problem of bringing his players back to earth. He said, "They may be on cloud 9 today. But Monday I'll bring them down. I'll run their rumps off. I may have to get a coat hanger to pull them back to earth. I'd rather go looking for a coat hanger than to go looking for shovel to dig them out of the ground. There's never been a Bowling Green team asked to do this — open at Purdue and then go to Miami of Ohio."

Somehow, Nehlen brought the Falcons back to reality, took them to Miami and won, 16-7. They were tied at Western Michigan the next week, 13-13, and then went to Toledo and won 19-8. Bowling Green was 3-0-1. And then the murderous schedule took its toll, the Falcons won only three of their last six games to end with a 6-3-1 record. But the Falcons' defense was 10th in the nation. Unfortunately, Nehlen's team finished second in the league again (4-1). Fans were beginning to wonder.

Nehlen faced another challenge the following year, too. His team had to open the season at Syracuse. Syracuse, under Coach Ben Schwartzwalder, was known for grind-it-out football and had produced great running backs like Jim Brown, Ernie Davis, Larry Csonka and Floyd Little. This might be a bigger challenge than Purdue the year before because this was Schwartzwalder's final year as coach of the Orangemen.

"I'm beginning to like playing a strong team in the opener," Nehlen said. "Sure, we may be running into a stacked deck. It's Coach Schwartzwalder's last year. I'm sure Syracuse has seen the film of our win over Purdue, so we're not going to sneak up on them. Our biggest defensive player weighs only 236 pounds. Syracuse will have a decided weight advantage."

On Sept. 15, 1973, Nehlen took his outmanned Falcons into Syracuse's ancient Archbold Stadium and walloped the Orangemen, 41-14. The Falcons rolled up 406 yards total offense and held Syracuse to 145, including 15 yards the first half.

Bowling Green President Hollis Moore proclaimed Nehlen the "Master of the Upset" and told a group of alumni, "We just might schedule Nebraska for our opener next year."

Schwartzwalder said, "We stunk the joint out today. Bowling Green is a very fine team and very well coached. But I think we made them look better than they were." Later that season a college team from Morgantown, W. Va., would squeeze past Schwartzy's final team, 24-14.

Bowling Green went on to post a 7-3 record, the most wins for a Nehlen-coached team in his six years as head coach. "I was beginning to think I was stuck on sixes," he said. But the team suffered conference defeats to Miami, Ohio U. and Kent State and finished in third place.

In 1974, the Falcons posted their fourth straight winning season and seventh in eight years under Nehlen with a 6-4-1 record. They traveled to Southern Mississippi and won, 38-20. That win was dedicated to Carlos Jackson, a Falcons' assistant coach who collapsed and died two days before the game. After that they went to San Diego State and played to a 21-21 tie. "They tied us, we didn't tie them," said Nehlen. But again a conference title eluded Nehlen. His team finished tied for fourth.

Provo, Utah, was the site of Bowling Green's opening game in '75. Brigham Young was defending Western Athletic Conference champion. Nehlen said, "It's just another tough opener against one of the better teams in the country. We're sorta getting used to that. We'll go out there and see what happens."

The Falcons went to Provo and pulled out a 23-21 win. The following week opened its home schedule against tough Southern Mississippi and won, 16-14. They ran their winning streak to six games — over Dayton, Western Michigan, Toledo and Kent State — before facing the always tough Miami Redskins. They lost, 20-17. That loss knocked Bowling Green out of the MAC title, doomed them to another second place finish — and sent them into tailspin that resulted in three losses in the last five games.

But it was Nehlen's best record (8-3). Another winning season. He was now the third winningest coach in Bowling Green history and the 24th winningest active coach in America with a 47-30-4 record.

The stage was set for the 1976 season. It promised to be, according to Bowling Green sportwriters, "one of the best ever in Bowling Green history, because the team will be potent, have a solid starter at every position in the line and have a wealth of talent in the backfield."

It was to be Nehlen's ninth and last season as head coach of the Falcons.

Don Nehlen starred in basketball at Canton Lincoln High.

His baseball skills earned him a place in the Canton Hall of Fame.

Football wasn't his first choice of sports, although it helped him earn a college scholarship.

Bill Diebel and youthful Nehlen as they appeared in the high school paper.

Prom night 1954 with his favorite girl, now his wife, Merry Ann.

His years as a player at Bowling Green were good ones.

That's "Pappy" on the far right, Don Nehlen's dad, the man who was Coach Nehlen's biggest fan. "Pappy" never lived to see his son's success as a head coach.

Engagement night 1957. Merry Ann and Don Nehlen.

Flat tops and drive-ins. Don Nehlen grew up in the fabulous fifties.

The "brown bomber," Don Nehlen's pride and joy.

Chapter Six

The boat was anchored in a quiet cove in Cumberland Lake near the southeastern border of Kentucky. It rocked gently as the two men fished. It was a warm, sunny day July, a time to relax and talk of things past and things to come.

Don Nehlen turned to Ken Schoeni, his best friend, and said, "You know, Schoens (Nehlen always called him that), we've had some good material at Bowling Green. We've upset some big teams. Yet, we just can't seem to get over the hump. I don't know. I think we've got a good team coming back this year. But you never know. If we get injuries, or something happens, well, I just might have to retire, sit out here in the boat, sun myself and learn how to fish."

Schoeni, assistant to the athletic director and in charge of all athletic facilities at Bowling Green, replied, "Don, what in the heck are you talking about? Come on, relax and fish." Schoeni thought it might be the beer talking, because he had managed to get Nehlen to drink a few — and Nehlen didn't drink. That didn't sound like the enthusiastic head coach Schoeni had grown to know and love.

The upcoming 1976 season had Falcon fans excited. Harold Brown, young sports editor at the Bowling Green *Sentinel-Tribune*, wrote that "Bowling Green will be impressive this year. Coach Don Nehlen's team will have no weak link — not one."

Schoeni had come to Bowling Green in '65, the same year that Nehlen had come back to take the defensive coordinator's job on Bob Gibson's staff. Schoeni had known Nehlen for more than 10 years. It had been "Schoens" who got Nehlen interested in boating. "I sold him my boat," said Schoeni. "Don would fish with me, but I really don't think he ever liked to fish. He was more into boating and water skiing.

"But I'll never forget that vacation before the '76 season when we were sitting in the boat on Cumberland Lake and Don said what he said. I've thought about it many times. He sounded like, well, like he was getting burned out."

What Nehlen was talking about wasn't being burned out. He was talking about what he thought was happening to the Bowling Green football program. A year earlier, he asked for a meeting with university President Hollis Moore (who died a few years later) and Dick Young, former Falcons' assistant coach who succeeded Doyt Perry as athletic director.

Nehlen asked for the meeting to find out whether there was a commitment to football. He was getting weary of bouncing around, of not having enough money to recruit, of getting home from recruiting trips at 3 a.m., because he couldn't afford a motel room, of doing odd jobs to earn extra money to augment his assistant coaches' salaries, of having to raise money for the program himself.

Nehlen had some proposals to present to his bosses. The meeting was set up — and the president didn't even bother to attend. Instead, he sent his vice-president. The handwriting was on the wall.

"I remember the meeting very well," Nehlen said. "I even asked basketball coach Pat Haley to attend. While I had been at Bowling Green, the school had gone through a number of basketball coaches. Everybody was getting fired, except me. I was one of the few coaches who hung on . . . by the skin of my teeth.

"Our program wasn't improving. The schedule was getting tougher. All we did was work harder and get less money. And we had more teaching load. Every year I lost some coaches because I couldn't pay them enough money. My highest paid assistant made only $14,000 and worked about 85 hours a week. And they all had to teach classes. They kept running out the door. I didn't blame them.

"At the meeting, the vice-president said to me, 'I don't know why you're so upset. You have tenure. Even if you don't coach football, you'll have a job here as a teacher. You'll have a job just like the track coach.'

"I said, 'If you guys really feel that way, then there's not much sense in this meeting at all.' Nothing was resolved. Anyhow, I felt it was just a matter of time until it caught up with me."

The time came that season.

As usual, the Falcons opened with another toughie — at Syracuse — and won, 22-7. It was another upset for the "Master of Upsets." After the game, Nehlen said, "Syracuse really puts a lot of money into its program. That we can compete with them is a credit to our players." The win was his 48th as head coach of the Falcons. He would win only five more.

The next week Nehlen's Falcons buried Eastern Michigan, 53-12, but it was a costly victory. The fear that Nehlen voiced to Schoeni that summer when they were fishing on Cumberland Lake came to pass — the team lost star fullback Dan Saleet for the year with a knee injury, and running back Dave Preston (now with the Denver Broncos) was injured and would miss a few games. "Life has not been a friend to Don Nehlen," wrote Brown. "Bowling Green will not be the same team without Saleet. He was 15th in the nation in rushing and an honorable mention All-American as a junior. Saleet and Preston gave the Falcons a potent backfield."

The third game was at home against San Diego State, and the Aztecs handed the Falcons their first loss, 27-15. Nehlen's team suffered more injuries. Nehlen said, "Our young men will just have to pick up the slack."

They did and squeezed past Western Michigan, 31-28. Next, they eked out a thrilling 29-28 win over Toledo by scoring twice in the final three minutes. And after that, they edged Kent State, 17-13.

After six games Bowling Green had a 5-1 record, but sportswriters criticized Nehlen for "not having the killer instinct."

Nehlen responded by saying, "They don't know what they're talking about. We have only three healthy offensive tackles on our entire roster. Preston has been hurt off and on all year. We're playing without five starters on defense. With all the injuries we've had, we're fortunate to be where we are."

Where they were was No. 1 in the nation in punt returns, eighth in total offense and No. 1 in the conference standings — and No. 1 in scoring.

Despite that, Nehlen was still criticized by sports editor Brown. Brown wrote, "In all honesty, the Falcons, even though they have been winning, have been outplayed. Bowling Green should be 2-2 in the MAC and not 4-0."

On October 23 at Oxford, Ohio, against old rival Miami, Nehlen probably sealed his fate as Bowling Green's coach. The Falcon faithful wanted a championship. Upsets of Purdue, Syracuse, Bringham Young and Southern Mississippi in recent years were OK, but it was the conference that was the No. 1 priority. And the faithful felt a win over Miami would be the clincher. It probably would have been.

But with 25 seconds to go in the game, and Miami leading, 9-7, Nehlen made a boo-boo the fans wouldn't forgive him for. The Falcons had the ball on the Miami one-yard line. Third down. Or, at least, that's what the down marker and scoreboard showed.

Nehlen said, "I remember looking at the scoreboard, and then at the down marker. I thought, 'Third down? That's not right. It's fourth down. Or, is it? Daggone, how did I lose a down?'

"Anyhow, I sent the field goal unit in. About that time several of my coaches told me it was third down. There was a lot of confusion. Now I wasn't sure what down it was. And we had to call our last time out to keep from being penalized for delay of game.

"In all the confusion I got a little confused myself and sent my offense back on the field. We ran a play and didn't make it. It didn't matter anyway because one of my linemen jumped offsides. That's when I learned it wasn't third down after all, but fourth down. We really screwed up. Funny thing is, I never have figured out why they didn't have the down marker or scoreboard right. Maybe that's what they call home field advantage. I don't know."

Nehlen was blasted in the newspapers the following week for the mistake. And the writers dug up "other mistakes" down through the years that had cost Bowling Green victories. Now, they were critical of his every move.

And when the Falcons lost the next game to Central Michigan, 38-28, Brown came out with a column titled: "It's Time For A Change." He wrote, "Admittedly, Don Nehlen has continued to turn out winning teams, but there's a difference between being a winner and being a champion. Nehlen is faithful and honest and injuries have hampered the team this year. But that's part of football. Interest in football has dropped off in recent seasons. Crowds this year have been disappointing. And it can all be traced to lack of a championship.

"This season went from impressive to embarrassing. For Nehlen's sake and the sake of Bowling Green State University football, it's time for a change."

Bill Estep, writer for the Bowling Green News, the school newspaper, wrote, "Somehow, the big ones always slip away from Nehlen."

Dean Roach, the former *Sentinel-Tribune* sports editor, said, "You have to understand, you had to win a conference championship at Bowling Green. It didn't matter how many games you won outside the conference. If you didn't win the title, you were a failure. It was as simple as that. Therefore, in the eyes of many, Nehlen was a failure. He certainly didn't earn the respect for the type of coach he was. In my opinion, he was treated unfairly."

After the "Time For A Change" story, the Falcons suffered their third straight loss, 31-26, at home to Ohio U. After that great 5-1 start, the team's record was now a disappointing 5-4.

Nehlen was assured of his eighth winning season in nine years (and the school's 21st in the last 22 years) the next week when Bowling Green snapped out of it with a 35-7 win over Southern Illinois. But it didn't matter. What mattered was that the Falcons, despite setting a conference total offense record with 4,425 yards, finished their MAC schedule 4-3 and way down in fifth place.

Then came the final game of the season on November 20 — a road encounter at Teenessee-Chattanooga.

Prior to the game, Nehlen was asked by sports editor Brown if he felt any pressure about his job. Nehlen replied, "No, I don't feel any pressure. We have a winning record and we've done it with a ton of injuries. I can't find half my team." His team had 11 players who had to have knee surgery and 14 others with broken bones.

The Falcons went into the game minus seven offensive regulars and four defensive regulars. They were a battered football team and they lost, 49-29, and ended the season 6-5. At halftime of the game, Bowling Green president Moore met with Athletic Director Young. Don Cunningham, who was the Falcons' business manager and assistant athletic director, said, "Moore was from Nashville and had brought a bunch of his Nashville friends to the game to see the Falcons play. I think the score of the game embarrassed him. Anyway, the gist of the conversation was that Moore told Young to start looking for a new coach."

Tom Kisselle, the former coach on Nehlen's staff and assistant athletic director that year, said, "Moore told Young he was going from Chattanooga to Florida and when he got back to Bowling Green he didn't want Nehlen there."

Young, now athletic director at Washington State, recalled, "Don's teams came within a whisker of winning three Mid-American Conference championships. But the big conference victory always seemed to get away from him. And there were some coaching errors that last season. President Moore and I did have a talk about the coaching situation. Moore was unhappy with the way things were going. I don't think that was any secret."

After the game, Moore came to the dressing room and sought out Nehlen. Nehlen recalled, "Moore said to me, 'I don't know, Don. I don't understand you guys. You tell me before the season you think you have a good team. You start out great, and then you're no good at the end. I don't understand that.'

Nehlen said, "I told Moore, 'Do you know who played for us in this game? Don't you know we have everybody hurt? They're all gone. We practically had our junior varsity playing for us today.'

"Then Moore said, "Well, I don't think you can coach anymore.'

"I said, 'The feeling is mutual. At least, we know where we stand with each other.' After that, Young told me he wanted to see me in his office as soon as we got back to Bowling Green. Right then and there I knew the fat was in the fire."

Wife Merry Ann recalled, "I didn't go on that trip. I was in bed asleep when Don got home. It must have been around 3 a.m. on Sunday morning. He climbed into bed and I rolled over and said to him, 'How are you doing?'

"He muttered, "Fine. I quit.'

"That really woke me up. I said, 'You did what?'

"He repeated, 'I quit. I'm quitting. This was it — my last football game at Bowling Green.' And he rolled over and went to sleep. I was wide awake the rest of the night."

The next day Nehlen got a call from Young and was told his football budget was being cut. "We didn't have a great budget to start with," said Nehlen. "That's when Young told me Moore didn't want me as a coach anymore. And that's when I told him of my decision to resign. I honestly don't think Moore would have fired me."

"I'll never forget our administrative staff meeting the first of that week," Kisselle said. "Young, a man I respect and admire, stood up and said, 'Don has resigned.'

"I stood up and said, 'That's bull! I just talked to him yesterday and I know what happened. I know you want it to come out in the newspapers like Don resigned of his own choice to make it look good. Dick (Young), we've been together a long time and you know this isn't right.'

"The thing that bothered me as a Bowling Green graduate was I knew what kind of a coach Don was and was going to be. He had done a heck of a job under the circumstances. He was loyal to the nth degree. Nobody ever worked harder. I can remember when I was on his staff all the nights we used to get into town from recruiting trips at

2, 3 and 4 a.m. — and have to get up the next morning to teach classes. I remember once we drove back from Cleveland in a blizzard and had to walk the last mile through three-foot snowdrifts. We must have been crazy.

"We used to work every Saturday because we had a game. We would work from Sunday before noon until midnight. We'd be back in the office the next day at 8 a.m. and work until about midnight . . . and do it the next day, and the next day, and the next day. On Friday we'd be with the team. On Saturday we'd play and start all over again on Sunday. We'd do all that work and some jackass looks at one or two plays and says, 'Why didn't you do this, or why didn't you do that?'

"Don was such a great person in the community. A church man. He was down to earth. He had no ego problem. He was able to get along with everybody. If they had just said to him, 'Don, you've been here all this time and done a heck of a job. We know during your years here that Miami had some of its greatest teams. So did Ohio University. And Toledo had probably its three greatest teams in its history. You have the second-best winning percentage in the history of the school, but you haven't won a conference championship.'

"If they had just said the truth, I could have lived with that. But in my thinking, Don Nehlen was railroaded."

On Monday, November 22, 1976, Nehlen told his staff they were all out of jobs. Assistant coach Russ Jacques, the former Bowling Green quarterback, said, "Don was very upset. He told us, 'I just resigned. And as of right now, we're unemployed. I don't know what's going to happen. I'm sorry.'"

"It was not an easy pill for any of us to swallow. We had beaten Purdue, Syracuse, all those teams. We had worked like dogs recruiting. But the biggest thing against Don's record at Bowling Green was he never won the MAC championship."

That night at the annual awards banquet, Nehlen told his team. It was an emotional banquet. He said, "Frustration, disappointments and a wave of negativism, which prevails on campus toward the football program, pretty much sum up my reasons for resigning." The Bowling Green News quoted Nehlen as saying, "The negative press never stops. It's always negative about me. I can't ever remember reading a good thing about me and I'm not an egotistical person. But that's not the reason I resigned. It's just very difficult to work in the situation that prevails here. If the team had been 9-2, I still would have been a loser in the minds of certain people. I never thought it would come to this."

Offensive tackle John Obrock said, "We're the ones who messed up, fumbled, had punts blocked."

Quarterback Mark Miller, the brother of Nehlen's first quarterback back at Canton South High School, said, "I'll never forget that night. A lot of players cried. I cried harder than anybody. He was an old family friend. My brother Tim played for him in high school. I came to Bowling Green because I wanted to play for him. I remember shortly after that, Harold Brown (the Sentinel-Tribune sports editor) talked about Don's leaving. He had tears in his eyes. He said he hated to see Don go and was sorry he had written what he had about him, but felt that was what people wanted."

After that, Nehlen seriously considered getting out of coaching and going into private business. "I had always been a positive-type guy and I still don't believe they would have fired me," he said. "But I was pressured into resigning, so I guess it essentially amounted to the same thing."

Athletic Director Young said, "Don would have been fired if he hadn't resigned. President Moore made that point clear."

"I do know," Nehlen added, "that it got to the point with all the problems at Bowling Green that I was not a very effective football coach. I could have stayed on as a teacher because I had tenure. But I didn't want the job. I was at the point in my career where I didn't even like football. The last few years at Bowling Green we were working harder and harder, getting less support, making less money. It was murder."

Schoeni, his boating and fishing friend, said, "We had some people here who were obsessed with winning the championship. I guess that's why you're in a conference. We were always No. 2 and No. 3 under Don. Some wrongfully tabbed him as a guy who would choke on the big game. Yet, he was known as the 'Master of the Upset.' I always thought that was sort of a contradiction. Don always had the capacity of taking an inferior team and playing a superior team and kicking their rear ends.

"He was very hurt by what happened to him that last year at Bowling Green. But he handled it with class. He didn't burn his bridges behind him. He didn't complain. But it was tough."

"I didn't agree with what they did to Don here," said Nehlen's old coach and mentor Doyt Perry. "I don't to this day feel he was a poor coach. And it wasn't because he was too young, either. Hell, he won some big games. You don't do that unless you have something on the ball. There's no question it hurt him having to resign. But he took it like a man. And he wasn't out of a job for long."

He wasn't. His unemployment lasted one month. That's how long it took for Perry to call his former assistant Bo Schembechler, the highly successful coach at Michigan.

"The first thing I did was talk to Don and ask him if he minded if I called Bo," Perry said. "I did. And I told Bo what had happened. At that time, Bo didn't have any openings on his staff. But he had a couple of assistants who were in consideration for head coaching jobs. One was Chuck Stobart, who was after the Toledo job."

Nehlen and Schembechler weren't strangers. Schembechler had been Perry's aide when Nehlen was a sophomore quarterback at Bowling Green. Later, he was head coach at Miami and recruited Nehlen's players when Nehlen coached Canton South and Canton McKinley. And

he was still coach at Miami in '68, Nehlen's first year as head coach at Bowling Green.

"Bo called me and said he didn't have an opening, but might have one soon," Nehlen said. "At that time, I wasn't sure I wanted to coach anymore. But Stobart got the Toledo job and Bo called again and offered me the backfield coaching position.

"He said, 'How soon can you be here?'"

"I said, 'In an hour.' "

The first thing that happened to Don Nehlen upon arriving in Ann Arbor was that he quickly learned how "the other half" lived. He found out what it was like to "actually have enough money" to go recruiting. Nehlen wasn't accustomed to that. He learned a few other things, too, things that completed his education as a football coach. He learned that most of the things he had done at coach. He learned that most of the things he had done at Bowling Green were right. He learned that Bowling Green football wasn't that much different from Michigan football. "I had received the foundation for my coaching the same place Bo did," Nehlen said. "Doyt Perry taught Bo. And Doyt Perry taught me."

He learned discipline from Schembechler, one of the master disciplinarians in the game. Nehlen admitted to having some discipline problems at Bowling Green. And he said, "I learned from Bo that with discipline you have a chance to win. Without it, you have no chance.

"I used to go to the office early so I wouldn't miss anything. Bo was able to get more out of people than anyone else I'd ever been around. I could have spent the rest of my coaching career with Bo. I learned a tremendous amount of psychology — how to handle players — from him."

And Nehlen learned what it was like to go first-class and to see a team treated first-class. And he learned that when a team is treated in a first-class manner, it usually plays the same way.

"Going to Michigan gave me a real shot of confidence," Nehlen said. "Suddenly, football became fun again. I always felt it should be."

It was another summer — 1978. Nehlen had been on Schembechler's staff for one year. He and Ken Schoeni were sitting in a boat again. This time they were on a small lake in the upper peninsula of Michigan.

Nehlen turned and said, "You know, Schoens, leaving Bowling Green was tough to take. I thought I was a good coach my last year there. When I got up to Michigan and worked with Bo, I knew darned well I was a good coach. I've learned some things from Bo, but mainly he helped me reaffirm in my own mind that most of the things I had been doing at Bowling Green were right.

"I know now that leaving Bowling Green was the best thing that ever happened to me, because it's going to help me down the road."

Chapter Seven

In Morgantown, W. Va., the rumors were flying. West Virginia University was in the market for a new football coach.

Nothing unusual about that.

At the end of every season, there are dozens of colleges and universities in the market for new coaches to breathe new life into their football programs. But this was unusual because it was late June. The 1979 football campaign was only a little more than two months away. Schools weren't usually in the market for coaches in the summer.

The Mountaineers were coached by Frank Cignetti, and he was recovering from a rare form of cancer. He had been seriously ill the preceding winter and was now undergoing chemotherapy treatments. Unless he got the go-ahead from his doctors, he was not going to be able to coach the team that year.

Wire service reports speculated that former Colorado Coach Bill Mallory, a former Bowling Green assistant coach who had applied for the Falcons' head job back in 1968 when Don Nehlen got it, was in the line for the job.

Meanwhile, that June, Nehlen was on his customary boating vacation on Portage Lake, just outside Ann Arbor, Mich.

Nehlen had heard the rumors. The grapevine in coaching circles is an amazing one. But he wasn't interested. He loved it at the University of Michigan. Even though he was an assistant coach and still had aspirations of being a head coach again, he was paid well. He and wife, Merry Ann, were happy. Son Danny and daughter Vicki were growing up. And Nehlen felt he had moved his family around enough.

Also, there was something exciting about being around Michigan Head Coach Bo Schembechler, watching the Wolverines play in front of crowds of 100,000-plus, winning and going to a bowl every year. In two years on the Michigan staff, Nehlen had been to two Rose Bowls.

But it wasn't a rumor. West Virginia Athletic Director Dick Martin was looking for a new coach, partly because the season was approaching and he didn't know whether Cignetti's health would permit him to coach. Martin thought he might need a coach. As he was looking, partly because in Cignetti's three previous seasons as head coach the team had been a losing one with records of 5-6, 5-6 and 2-9.

Mountaineer fans figured Cignetti was going to get the axe the year before. Instead, Athletic Director Leland Byrd resigned and Martin, former assistant commissioner of the Big Eight Conference, came on the scene.

Cignetti got his doctors' OK. He could coach the Mountaineers in the '79 season.

And although Martin didn't say it, it was common knowledge that if Cignetti didn't produce a winner, he was out.

A year earlier, West Virginia Gov. Jay Rockefeller had signed a bill authorizing construction of a new $20 million, 50,000-seat football stadium. There would be a new facilities building. The Mountaineers were looking to enter a new era. And that meant a new coach.

Meanwhile, back in Michigan, Nehlen put his boat away and launched himself into his work as assistant coach of the Wolverines. He was now Schembechler's quarterback and receivers coach. The season before he had coached Michigan's Rick Leach, who broke most of the school's passing records. Nehlen was having fun.

Construction had begun on the new WVU stadium. It would be ready for the start of the 1980 season.

Cignetti, although still undergoing chemotherapy, got his Mountaineers ready for the '79 campaign — a campaign that would end with another losing record (5-6) and would be his last.

A week after the Mountaineers played their final game in old Mountaineer Field and lost to arch-rival Pitt, 24-17, WVU traveled to Tempe, Ariz., to end the season against Arizona State. The Mountaineers had to win this one to salvage a winning season. There were few fans who figured that would happen. Few writers, too.

"Who will WVU get to replace Frank Cignetti?" wrote one. "West Virginia will probably hire an unknown assistant to replace Cignetti, because that's about all a school like WVU can attract," wrote another.

On November 17, the Mountaineers played Arizona State, scored first and then were routed, 42-7, as the Sun Devils rolled up an amazing 550 yards total offense against a hapless WVU defense. The verdict was sealed. Cignetti was fired, and Martin began the search for a new coach. Seventy-four men would apply for the position. None of the 74 would be Don Nehlen.

On December 7, Alan Robinson of The Associated Press reported that Martin had narrowed the candidates to four. He reported that they were ex-Colorado Coach Mallory, former West Virginia assistant coach Richard Bell, Pitt assistant Marv English and Gary Tranquill, offensive coordinator under Cignetti and a former assistant on Nehlen's Bowling Green staff.

Robinson was close.

A few weeks earlier, Huntington, W. Va., native Bob Marcum, athletic director at South Carolina, had called Martin and suggested he look into Nehlen's credentials. Marcum knew Martin from the Big Eight when he had been athletic director at Kansas. And he knew Nehlen back when he was an end coach on Nehlen's Canton McKinley High School staff. "You ought to check him out," Marcum told Martin. "And when you do, you will want to interview him. And when you interview him, you'd better be ready to hire him, because he'll be good."

Martin pursued it from there.

He said, "The more I checked into Nehlen's background, the more I was convinced he was a person we should interview."

Martin had set down certain criteria for the type of coach WVU was seeking. Martin wanted someone who would put the welfare of his players first, physically and academically. The new coach had to have a commitment to academics. He wanted someone who was personable and would relate well to the people of West Virginia. He definitely wanted someone who would go by the book, recruit well and have great enthusiasm. He wanted a coach who would recognize the potential at WVU at that time — with the new stadium and new facilities building — and develop it to his fullest. He wanted someone with integrity above reproach, a family man and a person who wouldn't embarrass the program or the university.

And the new coach had to be offensive-minded and someone who had some success on the Division I level.

In Nehlen, Martin found a coach who had been associated with only one losing season in 21 years as a coach (14 as a head coach and eight as an assistant) and six as a player. He found a man who had been a quarterback in high school and college. That fact meant the man would understand offense. And Martin found a man who had been associated with Bo Schembechler, one of the top disciplinarians and organizers in college football.

But Martin still hadn't contacted Nehlen. Instead, he busied himself doing his homework about him.

And one late November day in Ann Arbor, Mich., Schembechler called Nehlen into his office and asked, "Don, have you applied for the West Virginia job?"

Nehlen said, "No."

"Don't kid me," Schembechler said. The fiery coach of the Wolverines had other things on his mind — like getting his team ready to play in the Gator Bowl — and didn't want to go to the Jacksonvillie, Fla., bowl minus an assistant coach.

Nehlen said, "Bo, you know I don't kid. If I had applied for it, you would have been the first person I would have come to for help. Without you, I wouldn't have a chance of getting that job, or any job."

Schembechler said, "Well, some guy named Martin called here. He knows an awful lot about you. He knows how many games you won at Bowling Green. He knows the name of your wife, your children. Hell, he knows more about you than I do. It's been my experience that when someone knows everything about you, he's done his homework and is interested in you. Martin wants to know

if he can talk to you. I told him he could."

Nehlen was a little surprised. He hadn't applied for the job. Sure, he wanted to become a head coach again. He wasn't ignorant of the fact that West Virginia was looking for a man. And he had made a few inquiries. But he had not applied.

He went home that day and Merry Ann met him at the door and asked, "Who do you know in West Virginia?"

Nehlen said, "I don't know anybody. Why?"

She said, "Because some guy from West Virginia University is trying to get in touch with you. His name is Martin. Who is that?"

Nehlen said, "I don't know. I think he's their athletic director."

"Are you after that job?" she asked. "And will you tell me why?"

"First of all, I haven't applied for the job," Nehlen said. "But if the man wants to talk to me, I'm going to talk to him. It can't hurt anything."

Nehlen called Martin and Martin said, "I suppose you know we're looking for a football coach. I've looked into your background and like what I've learned about you. You have all the credentials we're looking for. Would you be interested in meeting me at the Pittsburgh airport so we can talk further?"

Nehlen agreed, but explained that he had a good job and loved it, and for the "first time in a long time enjoyed coaching football again." And he added, "If you are trying to solve some numbers game by including me in it, I'd appreciate it if you didn't put my name on the list. I have a lot of recruiting to do for Michigan. And we're busy getting ready to play in a bowl game."

"This is no numbers game," Martin said.

The meeting was arranged and took place at 10 a.m., November 28, in the Ambassador's Room of Trans World Airlines at the Greater Pittsburgh Airport.

Nehlen recalled, "I'll never forget that meeting if I live to be a million. We had just met and were sitting there talking. There was a television on in the corner of the room. And here was this guy from some Pittsburgh television station saying: 'Dick Martin, athletic director at West Virginia University, is expected to name Bill Mallory as new head coach of the Mountaineers in a day or two.'

"And there I was sitting there talking to Martin, supposedly about him being interested in me for the job. I said, 'Hey, Martin! I want you to know something. If you brought me down here for some blankety-blank runaround game, I'm going to get very angry. I know Bill Mallory. He's a heckuva coach and you'd get a heckuva guy. And I told you on the phone I didn't want to get involved in a numbers game.' "

Martin told Nehlen, "Everybody tells me I'm hiring Bill Mallory. That's not true. Not at this point. He is a very good candidate for the job. But I am looking at you, Mallory and a couple of other coaches."

Nehlen said, "OK."

The two men talked for about three hours. When they parted, Martin said, "I'm really interested in you. I'll be in touch." Nehlen caught a plane and went back to Ann Arbor.

One week later, Martin called Nehlen and asked if he could come back to Pittsburgh for a second interview. This one would be at the Holiday Inn near the airport. Nehlen said, "OK." This time Martin wasn't alone. He was accompanied by four members of the WVU athletic committee. Three other candidates for the job were there, too. Apparently Martin and the committee had narrowed it down to four.

All four were interviewed separately. After the interviews, Martin asked Nehlen where he would be in the next day or two if he needed to get in touch with him. Nehlen said, "I'm going to Louisville to recruit."

Martin then asked the committee members to go to their rooms, think about the candidates, and then write their choices on a slip of paper. In a few hours, before dinner, they would meet again and Martin would open the slips of paper.

"Don Nehlen was the unanimous choice of the committee," Martin said. "And he was my first choice, too. All that remained was to get the approval of university President Gene Budig. Since Nehlen was a unanimous choice of the committee, that didn't take long."

The next day, Dec. 7, the same day the wire service report came out that the candidates had been narrowed to four, Martin placed a call to Louisville, Ky., to the priests' quarters of a Catholic high school where Nehlen was staying (the school had a player Nehlen was trying to recruit). The phone rang. A priest said to Nehlen, "Coach Nehlen, there's a Mr. Martin who wants to talk to you."

Nehlen picked up the phone and said, "Hello, Dick. Well . . ."

Martin said, "You're it, Don."

And at about 5:30 p.m. on Dec. 7, 1979, Don Eugene Nehlen officially became the 30th coach in the history of West Virginia University football. A coach who at the time seemed to fulfill the earlier sportwriter's prophecy that "West Virginia will probably hire some unknown assistant because that's about all a school like WVU can attract." A coach that few, if any, Mountaineer fans had ever heard of.

Nehlen's hiring was supposed to have been a secret until the following Monday when a formal press conference would be held in Morgantown. The unfortunate thing about a secret is that when more than one person knows about it, it isn't a secret anymore. The news of his appointment leaked out the next morning.

Writers all over West Virginia went digging into their newspaper libraries to find out about this new coach. About all they came up with was: "Don Nehlen — Who?"

In the meantime, Nehlen called Merry Ann to tell her the news. "I got the West Virginia job," he said.

Merry Ann exclaimed, "West Virginia! I didn't even know they had a football team."

Nehlen said, "Mac (he always has called her Mac), I'm telling you I can see things happening down here. They're getting a new stadium, a new facilities building. Besides, it's not all that far away from Canton. We'll be near our folks."

Merry Ann said, "Ok, you're the boss." Her real thoughts were that her husband was just grabbing at straws to get a head coaching job again. They had discussed the possiblity that he might get the job, but she wasn't as enthused as he was. She had never been in West Virginia in her life. She didn't know anything about Morgantown. Daughter Vicki was in her senior year in high school. That would be a problem. And this would be their 13th move in 22 years of marriage.

Then she thought, "Don wouldn't just grasp at a straw. There must be more to that job." So, she prepared to get out the boxes again and start packing. Football coaches' wives never throw away boxes. And one thing Merry Ann was positive of, wherever her husband went, she would go, too.

Nehlen didn't know that much about West Virginia, either. The only time he had ever been in Morgantown was shortly after his first interview in the Pittsburgh airport with Martin. "A day or so after that," Nehlen said, "I was on a recruiting trip in Western Pennsylvania. I drove down to Morgantown, saw the Coliseum, the Fine Arts Building, the Towers dormitories and went out and took a look at the new stadium. That was it. Then, I turned around and headed back to Pennsylvania. Didn't even go to the main campus, or downtown.

"I didn't do a great job of homework about West Virginia. I talked to Gary (Tranquill) twice on the phone." Tranquill, who had been on Nehlen's staff at Bowling Green, was on Cignetti's WVU staff and was a candidate for the job.

"I said, 'Gary, what's the story down there?'

"He said, 'I think this can be a pretty good job, Don. The program is down right now. There is a lot of turmoil. Frank (Cignetti) is sick. There isn't much emphasis on strength and no strength program to speak of. The facilities are bad, but they are building new ones. But whoever gets the job is going to inherit a football team that has a few good players. Biggest problem is that for the most part the linemen are weak. I think there's a chance of winning here. And I don't have a job anymore now that Frank has been fired, so I applied for it. This is going to be a decent job for somebody.'

"I did know West Virginia had had some great teams in the past. And I knew the school was close to some great recruiting areas. And I always felt recruiting was one of my strengths.

"Anyhow, the next time I went to Morgantown was that Monday (Dec. 10) as the Mountaineers' new coach. You know, it was odd. You just don't get jobs that way. I didn't apply for the job. I didn't know Dick Martin. I didn't know President Budig. I didn't know very much about West Virginia. I had no one write me letters of recommendation. I had no one make a phone call for me. Bo never called Martin. Martin called him.

"Normally, you don't get a job coaching at a school when you don't know anyone there. And yet I ended up with the job. To this day, I don't know who all the other candidates were. I know Bill Mallory was one. I think

Wayne Hardin (former Temple coach) was one, but I'm not sure."

Martin said, "One thing that impressed me about Nehlen was that after he accepted the job, he said he wouldn't be able to come to work until after the Gator Bowl. Michigan was playing in the Gator Bowl and Nehlen said he had a commitment to Schembechler and Michigan — and he meant to honor that commitment. That confirmed what I had heard about him, that he was extremely loyal and dedicated."

Nehlen and Merry Ann flew to Morgantown on the West Virginia University plane for the press conference when he was officially introduced as the new Mountaineers' head coach. Merry Ann said, "I had the feeling that the moment I got on that plane that I was a West Virginian."

At the press conference, Nehlen was candid about his reasons for accepting the job. He said, "I've been asked why I took the job. well, I'll tell you why. I took it because I think West Virginia University's football program is a sleeping giant. Sure, I know nobody has ever won here consistently. But a few guys have won.

"I feel any time you are close to Ohio, Pennsylvania, New Jersey and New York, you have a chance, because there are a heckuva lot of good football players in those states.

"Now, I'm not going to kid you. If there wasn't a new football stadium and facilities building being built, there's no way I would have accepted the job. I wouldn't have even considered it. I've been that route. The old facilities here are terrible. Fans have complained because a few coaches have left (Jim Carlen and Bobby Bowden). Hey, if I had been in their shoes, I would have left, too.

"My first priority is to get the coaching staff assembled and on the job. I'll be calling the shots, but I'll be running back and forth between Ann Arbor and Morgantown. I'll be as busy as Santa Claus in the next few weeks."

One of the first things he did was hire a Michigan assistant coach, Dennis Brown, former Wolverines' quarterback, as his defensive coordinator. Brown said, "I was coaching linebackers at Michigan. It was a difficult decision for me to pick up and leave Michigan. I'm from Detroit. I played at Michigan, was a graduate assistant there and coached there for eight years. But I just felt it was time for me to go on and further myself professionally. Don offered me the chance to be a coordinator.

"I remember one day after the end of the 1979 regular season we were in the locker room. We'd just finished a practice session for the Gator Bowl. Don came up to me and said, 'D.B., I'm going for my second interview for the West Virginia job.'

"I was shocked, because I didn't know he had gone for the first one.

"He said, 'I think I'm going to get it. Are you ready to leave Michigan?' I think I said something about having to talk it over with my wife. And he added, 'Think about it and I'll call you later.' He did and told me he had the job.

"We went into Schembechler's office and Bo said to Don, 'Is this the guy you want to run your defense?'

"Don said, 'Yes.'

"And Bo said, 'Ok. But all I can tell you is, if you're defense isn't worth a crap, don't send him back to me.' And that's how I left Michigan."

"Getting Denny was a real plus for the program," Nehlen said. "He was always on the defensive staff at Michigan. I knew what kind of defense Michigan always played. And I knew I had to build one, to establish a defensive philosophy."

Nehlen hired Tranquill to run his offense. Tranquill, in addition to being with Nehlen at Bowling Green, had been on Woody Hayes' staff at Ohio State. And he called Russ Jacques, the guy he used to roust out of bed during two-a-day practices at Bowling Green. Jacques was coach of offensive backs and quarterbacks at Ohio University.

Jacques recalled, "Don contacted me right away. In fact, I think he contacted me before he got the job. You know, a coach applying for a head job has to start lining up his staff so that when he goes for the interview he has a game plan. Anyway, Don wanted to know if I would come with him. It took me exactly one second to say, 'Yes.' "

Others on Nehlen's first staff included Carl Battershell, a guard on Nehlen's first Bowling Green team; Mike Jacobs, who had been on Nehlen's Bowling Green staff; Bob Simmons, who had been an outstanding linebacker for Nehlen at Bowling Green; Bill McConnell, formerly defensive coordinator at Southern Illinois and Linebacker coach at Toledo; Bill Kirelawich, former Salem College linebacker. Donnie Young, WVU assistant coach under Cignetti, was retained as recruiting coordinator. And Nehlen hired his own equipment man, Mike Kerin, from Colorado.

Nehlen said, "Bo told me when I was at Michigan that if I ever got another head coaching job to make sure I ran the entire ship, to make sure everyone on my staff was hired by me, and that they are there because I want them there. That's what I did."

The next thing Nehlen did was meet with each of his new players. And the first questions he asked each was, "How are you doing academically?" And he told each, "I'm a new coach. I don't know anything about you. So, don't go hauling out any press clippings. We're all starting out fresh. I don't know you and you don't know me. I don't care if you were first string, or third string. You don't win games on what you did yesterday. You show me you can play, and you'll play.

"And I want you to know, nobody is as important to me as you. My office door will always be open. If you have a problem and want to see me, I don't care if I'm in a staff meeting, or talking to the governor, president of the university or the athletic director. I'l stop, because you come first with me."

And the next thing he did was establish his pattern for discipline. "I think I know how to coach," he said. "And I think I know how to recruit. And I know for sure I've learned how to maintain discipline. We will be a well-disciplined football team. I learned that from Bo Schembechler. If that guy doesn't like the way one of his players' ties his tie, well, the kid is in trouble.

"I don't know how many games we'll win. I can't answer that. Now, I'm not dumb. I know I gotta win. But I want to build a firm foundation and tradition. I want to build a program where the players love it, where it's fun. I want to have players who come in, graduate, go out and want to come back because they loved it and had fun.

"You do that with discipline. We will be a well-disciplined football team."

Chapter Eight

Don Nehlen eased his car onto Interstate 79. He was heading north out of Morgantown to Washington, Pa. There he would pick I-70 and head west to Ohio. He was on his first recruiting trip as the head coach of West Virginia University's football team.

He was heading toward his old stomping ground, eastern Ohio, the area rich in high school football talent and the one the Canton native knew best. And the first thing he did after getting on the interstate was to put a cassette tape into the dashboard tape player.

Was the new coach going to listen to music?

Not hardly. The new West Virginia University football coach didn't have time for that.

This first recruiting year would be tough. Nehlen had been hired on Dec. 7, but hadn't been able to take over the job until early January. National signing day was Feb. 20. There wouldn't be much time to recruit. If Nehlen and his new staff didn't get busy, they wouldn't recruit any players at all, much less any talented ones. And he knew at this late date, chances of signing good ones were slim at best.

Nehlen said, "We were starting out at a big disadvantage. We didn't know anything about West Virginia University. Dennis Brown, my new offensive coordinator, had spent all his life at Michigan. He didn't know anything about West Virginia. And how would I know anything about the school? I had spent my career at Bowling Green and Michigan.

"But we didn't have time to stick around and find out about the school. We had to hit the road."

And what Nehlen did was have recruiting coordinator Donnie Young, who had been assistant head coach on the former staff, go to an English professor and have him make a cassette tape about the university, about what it had to offer, about the city of Morgantown, about the state, everything.

Then, when Nehlen's coaches hit the road, they would be armed. "I gave each coach one of those tapes and told him to play it while he was in his car driving to wherever he was going to recruit," he said. "That way, at least he'd be able to speak with some intelligence to prospects about WVU. And that's how we learned about the school — by playing cassettes in our cars while we were on the road. It was a crash course."

That crash course didn't show immediate results. On national signing day, Nehlen had signed only eight players. But he would eventually sign 26. Those 26 signed that winter of 1980 included such future WVU stars as Rich Hollins, Tim Agee, Steve Newberry, Bill Legg, Kurt Kehl,

Rick Walters, Dave Preston and Steve Hathaway.

"We were lucky," Nehlen said. "At that time, I wasn't jubilant. It had been such a rush job of recruiting. I had been in the business long enough to know you didn't evaluate your first recruiting class until three years later. That's when you know whether you did, or whether you didn't."

Nehlen's first WVU spring practice began in late March. The new coach pulled no punches. He described his Mountaineers as "a very average football team" that didn't have "nearly enough football players." And he added the team was "one of the weakest he had ever seen."

"Somehow, we've got to get stronger," he said. "I thought to myself that first spring that this West Virginia team was about like one of my teams at Bowling Green as far as personnel went. Sure, I inherited some players like Delbert Fowler, Fulton Walker, Robert Alexander, Walter Easley, Cedric Thomas and quarterback Oliver Luck. Those guys were better than guys I had at Bowling Green. But the rest weren't. I knew I had a long way to go."

The construction crews working on the new stadium out near the WVU Medical Center had a long way to go, too. They were working against a deadline — Sept. 6 when the Mountaineers were scheduled to open against Cincinnati. The stadium had to be ready.

A month before the opener, the AstroTurf still hadn't been put down. Paving around the new structure was non-existent. There were piles of dirt everywhere and not a blade of grass to be seen. There was even talk of moving the opener back to Nov. 29 in case the stadium wasn't ready.

"All I know is they tell me it'll be ready," said Nehlen. "I hope they know what they're talking about."

The team couldn't get on the new field. It had to practice at the old stadium. Nehlen posted guards on the gates and put up "Closed Practice, Keep Out!" signs.

"Too many distractions," he said. "Why, there were girls jogging around the field and everything. They may not have distracted the players, but they sure distracted the coaches."

A few day before the game, Gov. Rockefeller addressed a fund-raising banquet in Clarksburg and said, "There are few persons I have met in my 42 years who have impressed me as much as Don Nehlen has. The coming of Don Nehlen and the first-rate facilities are a happy coincidence."

Meanwhile, Nehlen knew the tension on his team was

building. He could sense it by the way practices were going.

One afternoon to ease the tension, he arrived at practice by helicopter. He said, "It was just a gimmick to loosen up the team. Really, it was because I am a stickler for being on time and that was the only way I could bypass city traffic and make it to practice on time myself. You know what I mean?"

Opening day finally rolled around. Sept. 6, 1980. Don Nehlen's first game as new coach. The first in the new arena. And hopefully, the first of a new era of Mountaineer football.

The stadium? Well, it was ready for a game. That was about all.

But the artificial turf was down. And there were 50,000 seats. Recent rains had hampered the finishing touches. The locker rooms weren't ready and wouldn't be for months. Players had to tramp through the mud between the partially completed facilities building to the field.

The night before someone had remembered they had forgotten to put up a flagpole. One was hastily put up. After all, what would a game be without the National Anthem and the raising of the flag?

At 1:30 p.m. on game day, a crowd of 50,150, largest ever to see a football game in the state of West Virginia, jammed into the new arena. WVU officials didn't expect that many. There had been a last-minute foul-up on tickets. The Mountaineers' ticket office was accustomed to handling ticket requests for games in 35,000-seat old Mountaineer Field, not for games in the new one.

Singer John Denver was there. So was Governor Rockefeller.

There was a ribbon-cutting ceremony and pre-game speeches.

Nehlen said, "That was probably the most difficult football game I've ever prepared for. The game had more pressure for me than any game I'd ever been in. It was the opening of the new stadium. It was my first as West Virginia coach. I knew I didn't have a real good football team. In fact, I didn't know what kind of team I had. It was a carnival-like atmosphere.

"And it was the first time in my coaching career I ever had to do something like that before a football game. I had to go out and cut a ribbon, or something, and I had to talk to the fans and student body. I didn't want to do it, but I felt it was important.

"If you knew my mental makeup before a game and how I try to prepare a football team . . . well, it was just very difficult for me to go out there when my team was in the locker room."

Nehlen knew, too, that all he had heard all summer was talk about 'THE' opening game in the new stadium against the University of Cincinnati. "It was like, man, if we lost this game, we're going to let down the entire world," Nehlen said.

Denver sang "Country Roads." The Mountaineer Marching Band performed. The flag was raised. It was time to play ball.

And Cincinnati scored first, on a 45-yard field goal. Nehlen's first WVU team trailed, 3-0. When that happened, Nehlen thought, "I didn't think we were going to be very good, but I thought we'd certainly be better than this."

The Mountaineers were. Robert Alexander rushed for 187 yards and scored two touchdowns. Oliver Luck completed 10 of 15 passes for 138 yards and two touchdowns, one to Thomas. Walter Easley rushed for 89 yards and scored twice.

Going into the fourth quarter West Virginia led, 35-13, and won, 41-27.

Nehlen said, "When that game was over I felt like a 100-pound weight had been lifted from my shoulders. Now, I didn't think we played particularly well. I knew Cincinnati was just an average team. Yet, it scored 27 points on our defense. That wasn't a good sign. I knew if Cincinnati could score that many, what in the heck would the rest of the teams on our schedule do? I still didn't know what kind of team I had.

"I was just happy we scored more than Cincinnati did."

Nehlen's first road game as WVU coach loomed ahead — at Colorado State. This was the game in which Nehlen first demonstrated his ability of being able to work on his players' minds.

The new coach knew that two seasons before West Virginia had gone out to Fort Collins, Colo., and had been humiliated by the Rams, 50-14. "We had several guys on the team who played in that game," Nehlen said. "I just planted a seed in their minds so they would remember how Colorado State had embarrassed them. And I told them that we weren't going to die in that Rocky Mountain altitude. Instead, I said, 'We're going to take it to them in the second half.'"

"I knew Colorado State was just an average team. Trouble was, I wasn't sure we were much better than that. And I was afraid Colorado State might have more speed. They had just beaten Air Force, 21-9."

Nehlen's mental preparation of his team worked because his Mountaineers rolled to a 52-24 victory. Luck led the offense by passing for 269 yards (12 of 20) and three touchdowns, two to Thomas. The Mountaineers had 615 yards total offense and after two games were averaging 529 yards and 46 points. Only two teams in WVU history had ever scored more points in the first two games.

"A lot of folks thought our offense was great," said Nehlen. "It wasn't. And a lot of people thought our defense was horrible. It wasn't. We weren't a great team. Far from it. But our kids were playing with great emotion and enthusiasm. And I knew as long as we did that, we'd cause folks some problems."

The Mountaineers returned home on Sept. 20 for the second game in the new stadium. A crowd of 48,048, second-largest ever, was on hand to see Nehlen's 2-0 team face always tough Maryland, which was also 2-0.

Nehlen suffered his first defeat at WVU, 14-11. "But we showed plenty of fight," he said. "We scored our only touchdown with 59 seconds to play and trailed by three points. Had we recovered that onside kick, we might have pulled it out. I learned that day that our kids have plenty of fight. Unfortunately, the game was played in the trenches. Maryland was stronger in those trenches than we were. I mean, Maryland was a strong, physical football team. I knew we had to get stronger.''

Richmond was next and a home crowd of only 40,847 fans turned out on a sunny, 70-degree afternoon to see WVU battle the Spiders.

''Yeah, we clobbered them,'' said Nehlen, ''thirty-one to twenty-eight! Did it with a touchdown in the final 19 seconds.

''Our special teams broke down. We let Richmond return the opening kickoff 94 yards for a touchdown. That gave them the spark they needed. Also, Oliver Luck had a bad ankle.''

It was in that game that Nehlen displayed the discipline he had learned under Schembechler at Michigan.

WVU junior wide receiver Darrell Miller, the guy teammates called ''Coast-to-Coast'' and one of the leading receivers, came off the field on a fourth down. The problem was that Miller wasn't supposed to come off. He was on the punt team, too, and was supposed to stay out there.

Punter Curt Carion took a head count of the team in the huddle and said, ''Uh oh, we've only got 10 men out here.'' He signaled to the bench.

Now, unfortunately, Nehlen didn't have time to check and see who was missing. He had to waste a time out.

Then, he found out who the culprit was. It was Miller, who was sitting on the bench rubbing his leg.

Nehlen walked over to him and asked, ''What's the matter son?''

Miller said, ''My leg is sore, coach.'

Nehlen replied, ''I don't care if your leg is sore. If you ever do that again, turn in your uniform.'' And he turned and walked away.

Afterward, a writer asked him, ''You really wouldn't have made Miller turn in his uniform, would you? He's one of your top receivers.''

Nehlen snapped, ''Yes sir. Right now!''

And that was the end of that. Miller never did it again. Neither did anyone else.

The Mountaineers won the next week and improved their record to 4-1 with a 45-21 homecoming victory over Virginia before a crowd of 45,000. Two WVU scores were made by the defense. Delbert Fowler picked a fumble out of the air and returned it 14 yards for a TD, and future All-American Darryl Talley intercepted a pass and ran it in from 30 yards out.

''Fans were getting excited,'' Nehlen said. ''But I wasn't. I knew what we had ahead of us. It was going to be murder, maybe disastrous.''

What was ahead was a mid-season trip to Hawaii to play the University of Hawaii Rainbows, followed by back-to-back games with Pitt, Penn State and Virginia Tech.

Nehlen said, ''I was opposed to the Hawaii trip from the day I took the job. I remember, the first thing I said to Athletic Director Dick Martin was, 'Dick, we've got to

work and try to change this Hawaii trip. We have plenty of time. Try and get rid of it. Get rid of that trip to San Jose State next year, too. Long trips to open a season or in the middle of a season are brutal. Let's see if we can't get trips closer to home.''

But Martin felt the Hawaii trip was too far in motion. Too many alumni had made plans to go and were excited about it. WVU and Nehlen were committed to play at Hawaii.

''The year after I left Bowling Green,'' Nehlen said, ''Denny Stoltz, the new Bowling Green coach, had to take the Falcons to Hawaii during the season. They were beaten 41-21.

''Going to Hawaii for the final game of a season is one thing. That would be a great way to end a season. But to go in the middle of the season? That was crazy.

''There was the problem of preparing a team to go. We had to go a week early. That meant players would be out of classes a week. We had to take a scout team. Had to have a team to run Hawaii plays. That meant our traveling squad went from 50 to 55 players to 75 or 80. That was just 25 more headaches for me to worry about.

''We were going to a place that would be like a bowl atmostphere. We would be staying in a fancy hotel. There would be the beaches, the girls, the sun. Too many distractions. And we were going through six times zones. The game wouldn't start until 1:30 a.m. our time and end about 4:30 our time.

''Also, I knew Hawaii was traditionally tough out there. Ask Nebraska and Oklahoma. They had gone out there and managed to win, but they'd won by only a single point, or a touchdown. And I knew for sure we didn't have a team like Nebraska or Oklahoma.

''The other problem was when we had to take 75 or 80 kids, that meant we had to leave 20 or 25 at home. How do you tell a kid he can't go to a place like Hawaii with his teammates? I didn't like to have to do that. I've always believed on a trip like that, you either take all your players, or you just take your travel squad. It was a bad situation.''

The Mountaineers weren't going to make any money, either. The contract with Hawaii called for them to get only a $35,000 guarantee, although Martin did try to no avail to get Hawaii to up it. That $35,000 wouldn't pay for the food. It was going to cost WVU nearly $170,000 to make the trip. ''No matter which way you sliced it, we were going to lose a bundle,''said Nehlen. ''I felt that game was a cancer on our schedule.''

The Mountaineers flew to Hawaii on Monday and worked out in Aloha Stadium the next afternoon in 100-degree heat. After the workout, Nehlen let his players go to the beach for two hours — period. The next day he let them go to the beach for two more hours. ''That's the end of the beach for them,'' he said.

''I know why Hawaii wins 90 percent of its home games. Miles and miles of beautiful beaches. Scads of beautiful girls in skimpy bathing suits. I'm afraid my kids don't have their minds on football. I think they think they're here on a vacation, and this is no vacation.''

It wasn't, either. West Virginia took a 3-0 lead at the

start of the second quarter on an 18-yard field goal by Steve Sinclair. Then, on the next possession quarterback Luck suffered a concussion and had to leave the game. Despite the loss of Luck, the Mountaineers held a 6-0 halftime lead, thanks to another Sinclair field goal.

Hawaii tied it with a third-quarter touchdown (the extra point was missed). In the meantime, Luck had regained his senses. And Nehlen, with the doctor's OK, sent Luck back into the game. He promptly engineered a 78-yard drive, climaxed by a six-yard scoring pass to tight end Mark Raugh for a 13-6 lead. But Hawaii came right back with an 80-yard drive to tie it again.

A Robert Alexander fumble with 1:30 to play in the game gave the Rainbows possession at the WVU 32, and four plays later, they took a 16-13 lead on a 40-yard field goal. And the game ended when a WVU field goal attempt was blocked.

"If Luck hadn't gotten hurt," Nehlen said, "we would have won the game. When he was in there, we moved the ball at will.

"Then after the game, we had to go to bed, get up early and catch a plane and fly back through those time zones. We landed in Pittsburgh at 9:30 at night and didn't get back to Morgantown until 11:30. Sunday was over and we hadn't done a single thing to prepare for our next game. And that was at Pitt."

Normally, by 11:30 Sunday night Nehlen and his staff have more than half of the next game's game plan set. This time they hadn't done a thing. The coaches were tired. So were the players. And jet lag hadn't set in yet.

Nehlen said, "We came back to work the next morning and my coaches were still tired. Their eyes were red and burning. They couldn't look at film. After a few hours, I sent them home. We still didn't have a game plan.

"And we hadn't practiced, either. We couldn't practice. My team was dead tired.

"That trip to Hawaii in the middle of that '80 season was just a terrible thing to do to a football team. Oh, it was great for the alums. They went over there, sat around the pool and drank. But it was a terrible situation for a bunch of young athletes."

When Nehlen and his staff finally got around to looking at films of Pitt, the 11th-ranked Panthers looked exactly like what they were — a tremendously talented team. headed by senior All-American linebacker Hugh Green and sophomore quarterback Dan Marino, who Nehlen called "the classic type quarterback with a shotgun for an arm that the pros are looking for."

But Nehlen added, "I'm not as worried about this game as I was last week's game at Hawaii. We can't match Pitt in talent, but I know our players will play with great effort."

Nehlen was right about one thing. West Virginia didn't match Pitt in talent. And he was wrong about the other. The Mountaineers didn't put forth great effort. The Panthers scored seven points in the first quarter and 28 in the second and cruised to a 42-14 victory. It was WVU's second straight defeat and sent its record to 4-3.

"This was supposed to be a backyard brawl," said

Nehlen. "I thought our players would be fired up. Turnovers (two interceptions and two fumbles) in the second quarter killed us."

Next was Penn State. The only thing in the Mountaineers' favor was that the game would be at Mountaineer Field. A crowd of 49,194 turned out despite steady rain, gusting 25-mile-an-hour winds and 50-degree temperature to witness the battle.

This would be Nehlen's first introduction to the WVU-Penn State series. He had checked into the one-sided rivalry. He knew the Mountaineers hadn't beaten the Nittany Lions since 1955. That was when he was a skinny, sophomore quarterback at Bowling Green. He knew that none of his current Mountaineers had been born when WVU last beat Penn State.

The Lions came in with a 5-1 record and were paced by West Virginian Curt Warner, the Pineville star a former WVU assistant coach once described as "not good enough" to play for the Mountaineers. Warner was averaging 12.5 yards per carry for Penn State. And quarterbacking the Lions was a youngster named Todd Blackledge, son of Ron Blackledge, former assistant on Nehlen's staff at Canton South High School.

Backing up Blackledge at quarterback was a kid named Jeff Hostetler.

Right off the bat, the Mountaineers messed up the coin flip. Nehlen instructed co-captains Fulton Walker and Gordon Gordon to "take that wind" if they won the toss. He reasoned, "Since it was raining and the wind was gusting, he wanted the wind." Also, under those conditions, he figured the Lions just might make a mistake.

Walker and Gordon said, "Heads," and the coin came up heads. The co-captains insisted they told the referee they would "take the wind." The ref insisted they said, "We'll kick off."

Anyhow, Penn State not only got to receive, but also got its choice of ends of the field — and took the end with the wind at its back.

Nehlen blew his stack and rushed onto the field to complain. Penn State Coach Joe Paterno rushed out to protect his interests and told the ref, "You made your decision. Now stick to it." The ref did. It was an advantage that enabled the Lions to walk off at halftime with a 10-0 lead.

The Mountaineers came out in the second half and scored on a safety and a 23-yard TD pass from Oliver Luck to Billy Evans to make it 10-8. Momentum seemed to be swinging their way. The defense was playing well. Warner had gained 83 yards, but it took him 29 carries to do it. Up to that point, Warner had not been a factor. But he was on the ensuing kickoff. He took the ball at his 12, cut to his left and went 88 yards to score. That proved to be the winning tally and Penn State went on to win, 20-15.

Hostetler played briefly and completed one of three passes for 15 yards.

Afterward Nehlen said, "I know that was our third straight loss and we're now 4-4. But our kids played extremely well. It's the best they've played all year. I don't know what happened on the toss of the coin. I told our co-captains what I wanted. It didn't work out that way. You know, sometimes when you talk to your players, you think they hear you, but they don't. One of these days it'll turn my hair gray.''

A road game against Virginia Tech was next. Tech was always tough for WVU, particularly on that windy plateau in Blacksburg. It was a humiliating 34-11 defeat, WVU's fourth in a row. The Mountaineers' record was now a dismal 4-5. Oliver Luck completed only three of 11 passes the first half and for the game the offense managed just 226 yards. Tech rolled up 420.

"Ollie is uptight," Nehlen said in the locker room after the game, "but he isn't the only one. The whole team is uptight. I guess it's because we're losing and the kids are afraid of making mistakes. When players are trying as hard as ours are, they can't execute. What's the reason for that? Hey, I've coached 21 years and I don't have the answer. If I did, I could make a million dollars.

"Right now, we have no spark, no consistency, nothing. Our injury list is growing each game. Depth was a problem at the start of the season and it really is now. It won't change. Playing a 12-game schedule without an open date doesn't give us a chance to get anybody well.''

Some fans were concerned that the Mountaineers, despite a new coach, were about to take a swan dive. Since 1976, including a disastrous 2-9 season in '78, West Virginia teams had been 16-6 in the first half of the season and 4-16 the second half.

Nehlen spent all of that next week preaching to his players to "relax and have some fun" when they went to Philadelphia to play Temple. "And quit worrying about losing," he said. And on Nov. 8, the Mountaineers went into Veterans Stadium relaxed and outlasted the Owls, 41-28, to end that four-game losing streak.

Luck was his old self again as he completed 20 of 25 passes for 314 yards and four touchdowns — two to Cedric Thomas, who set a school record for most TD receptions for a single season (9) and a career (20).

"We finally relaxed and got the monkey off our backs," said a happy Nehlen. "Ollie threw the heck out of the ball. When he does that, we can beat a lot of teams.''

Next it was Rutgers at Rutgers. The Scarlet Knights were 6-3 and had visions of beating WVU and landing a bid to a minor bowl. Nehlen wasn't too happy about playing in tiny 23,000-seat Rutgers Stadium. He wanted the game switched to the 76,500-seat Meadowlands. "No way," was the word from Rutgers. The Knights wanted to get the Mountaineers on their home turf.

Nehlen felt his team was "in the middle of the stream.'' He said, "We're 5-5. We have two games to play. I'd like to win both. But I darned sure want to win one. I don't want a losing season. Neither do my players.''

An unheralded sophomore named Allen Moreland came up with two key interceptions in the final two minutes of the game, and the Mountaineers came away with a 25-15 win. It assured them a non-losing season, their first since the 9-3 Peach Bowl team of 1975. Fullback Walter Easley gained 94 yards and scored twice and Luck was on target for another score (15 out of 26 passed for 194 yards).

"Two weeks ago everybody was selling this team down the river," Nehlen said. "I tried to tell folks we didn't have a great team. But it ain't bad, either. This was a big win for us. Make no mistake, Rutgers was a pretty good team — and thought it was going to a bowl. I'm proud of the way our kids sucked it up and pulled this game out. Now, there's no way anyone can say they are losers.''

Nehlen's first team ended its season on Nov. 22 before the smallest home crowd of the year (34,441) by losing to Syracuse, 22-7. The Mountaineers went into the game minus defensive ace Fulton Walker and top receiver Cedric Thomas. During the game, seven more Mountaineers joined them on the injury list, including Luck, who went out in the first half with a dislocated shoulder, and middle linebacker Dave Preston, who went out with an injured knee.

"Our players were dropping like flies," said Nehlen. "We were to the point where we only had one healthy defensive lineman. He was a freshman (Dwayne Jones). We put him in and he got his leg broke on the first play. After that we had to put an offensive lineman in to play defense. We just ran out of football players. I was just hoping somebody in the press box would let the clock run.

"The end of this season was a blessing.

"But I said back in early October that the trip to Hawaii would be murder. We probably wouldn't have beaten Pitt anyway, but we might not have lost at Virginia Tech . . . and might not have lost to Penn State, either. A trip like that right smack in the middle of a season? Wow! That cost us in more ways than money.

"And I said prior to the start of the season that this team wasn't strong enough and was just an average team trying to get better. But I will guarantee you one thing, in 1981 this West Virginia football team is going to be stronger.

"That's a promise.''

Chapter Nine

It was fourth down.

Ten yards to go.

Only 4:45 was left in the game.

The West Virginia football team trailed Maryland, 13-10, and was going to have to give up the ball.

At that moment in the second game of the 1981 season, the hostile crowd in Maryland's Byrd Stadium let go with an ear-splitting roar. The Terrapins had stopped the Mountaineers. West Virginia would have to punt, and all the favored home team had to do was make a couple of first downs and the game would be over.

Coach Don Nehlen's Mountaineers pleaded with him to let them "go for it." After all, they were at the Maryland 48, and with veteran Oliver Luck at the controls, chances were better than 50-50 he would complete a pass for the first down. He had already completed 24 of 47 for 255 yards and one touchdown. Why, that was more than Nehlen threw (and completed) one entire season when he was a quarterback at Bowling Green in the mid-50's.

Nehlen ignored the pleas. He said, "Punt the ball."

His players pleaded again, "Let's go for it. We can make it, coach."

Nehlen answered loud and clear, so there would be no misunderstanding, "I said PUNT THE BALL!"

More than a few of the Mountaineers gave him funny stares. Hundreds of WVU fans who had come to College Park on that clear and cool Sept. 19 afternoon were convinced the second-year head coach had a few marbles missing.

Nehlen recalled, "I'm sure the fans thought I didn't know what I was doing. And I could tell by the stares from the players that they thought their coach was a little loony."

But the coach knew if WVU went for it and didn't make it, Maryland would take over near midfield and could conceivably put more points on the board. Also, he knew if the Mountaineers punted, there was a chance Maryland might mishandle it. Even if the punt wasn't mishandled, there was time for the WVU defense to hold the Terps and get the ball back.

There was time. And it was no time for Nehlen and the team to gamble, not when they were still in the game. One score and they could win.

Nehlen's punting team huddled around him. He said to punter Jody McKown, "Don't punt it into the end zone. Make their guy handle the ball."

And he said to the rest of the special team, "We have to get the ball back. Now, I'm telling you, they are going to

make a mistake. Go down on this punt like you've never gone down on a punt before. And just watch, their guy will mess it up. We'll get it back and score."

West Virginia punted. Maryland's punt returner took his eye off the ball to glance at the horde of Mountaineers bearing down on him, and fumbled the ball. West Virginia's Rich Hollins recovered at the Maryland 12-yard line. Four plays later, Luck sneaked into the end zone for the winning score.

West Virginia won, 17-13, and the following Tuesday appeared in the top 20 of one wire service's poll. The Mountaineers, tied for 20th with Arkansas, had made its first appearance in the polls in six years.

"That was the day our football team grew up," said Nehlen. "That one play did it. They began to believe in my philosophy. We won by saying we were going to, and then going out and doing it. We got a break and capitalized on it. When their guy fumbled the ball, we had 10 guys around him ready to pounce on it.

"And it was the first time since I came to West Virginia that we won a game with our defense. Always before West Virginia had won with offense. This time we won by stopping our opponent. Maryland had been to eight bowls in recent years. We hadn't been to the toilet bowl and yet they got their only touchdown when we were penalized half the distance to the goal, all the way back to our 13, for illegally kicking a punt. Jody McKown booted the ball only 11 yards into the wind and it started rolling back toward our goal. Dennis Fowlkes kicked the ball out of bounds.

"The refs were right in calling the penalty, but I thought they were going to penalize us all the way to the Maryland locker room."

After the game, Nehlen huddled with his jubilant players in the locker room and told them, "See what can happen when you play every play like it's the last play? See what happens when you never look at the clock? It was dynamite!"

He explained, "I had been trying for a year to convince them if they did that, things would work out in their favor when the dust settled. The Maryland game proved that. Before the game I think I had a bunch of semi-believers. I didn't have any semi-believers after that."

It was a game Nehlen would bring up again and again in pre-game and halftime talks in the ensuing weeks.

A week earlier, the Mountaineers opened the season 2½ point underdogs at Virginia and whipped the Cavaliers, 32-18, in 100-degree heat. "The early part of the schedule was tough," Nehlen said. "We had to play our first two games on the road, go home to play Colorado State, go to Boston College and then come back home to play Pitt."

The Virginia win was costly. Wide receiver Darrell Miller, the kid Nehlen disciplined the year before for forgetting he was on the punt team, caught six passes for 92 yards in the first half. On his seventh catch, a 23-yard reception on a third-and-13 situation, Miller suffered a knee injury and was lost for the rest of the year. He was the eighth Mountaineer to injure a knee (and the fifth to have surgery) and the Mountaineers were only a little more than one-half of the way into the season.

"The temperature the day we played in Charlottesville was unbelievable," Nehlen recalled. "It must have been 118 degrees on the AstroTurf. It was brutal. I wasn't sure how my kids would hold up in that heat."

It turned out the Mountaineers, except for Miller, whose injury had nothing to do with heat, held up very well. It was the coach who didn't.

"I almost passed out," Nehlen said. "The soles of my feet were burning from standing on that turf. I remember, Gary Tranquill (offensive coordinator), who was up in the press box, told me on the phone early in the fourth quarter, 'Don, we can get two or three more touchdowns.'

"I said, 'Jiminy Christmas, Gary, we're leading 32-10. I don't want any more touchdowns. I just want to run out the clock and get out of here before I melt. I'm wringing wet with sweat. I think I've got blisters on my feet. I don't think you're aware of how hot it is.'

"Tranquill said, 'Ok, you're the boss.' Then I heard him say to someone in the press box, 'Pass me another Pepsi.'

"Here I was dying in the heat and he was up there in the press box drinking ice cold Pepsis and wanting us to stretch the game out so we could score some more points."

To make sure that didn't happen, Nehlen instructed his quarterback not to throw any passes and instructed his co-captains and coaches not to call any timeouts. "I told them not to do anything but run the ball," he said. "And I think I said something to the effect that I didn't care what the score was as long as we were ahead.

"I know they thought I was loony — although, not nearly as loony as they thought I was when I ordered that punt against Maryland."

But the big play on the punt against Maryland put WVU over the hump. Over the winter Nehlen had sold his players on the theory that they could win if they got stronger. It was the first winter the Mountaineers were in their new weight room in the facilities building. And they made the most of it.

They didn't run.

They didn't do quickness drills.

They pumped iron.

Nearly every player added 15, 20 and 30 pounds. And every player increased his strength by at least 20 percent. Nehlen said, "I know that sounds like a lot. But it wasn't, not when you consider where we were starting from. Oh, we had a couple of guys who could bench press about 350

pounds. But not one of our offensive linemen could bench over 315. It was about the same with our defensive linemen. We had to develop a strength attitude."

In addition to talking about a strength attitude, Nehlen constantly harped that "strength builds confidence" and "confidence means you can win." He wanted each of his players to look in the mirror and feel good about himself, because he knew when 100 young athletes, all wearing the same color jersey and same color helmet, feel good about themselves, they would win more often than not.

The difference was obvious in drills that spring. The Mountaineers were stronger. There were more pad-crunching collisions on the field, more guys banging each other around. Nehlen wasn't beaming, because he knew the team had a long way to go. But he was smiling, because he knew how far it had come. He could tell his players enjoyed throwing their newly added weight around.

"That's why when we came from behind to beat Maryland the way we did," said Nehlen. "I could now stand up in front of my players and say, 'See, what did I tell you? It worked. You got stronger and more confident. I told you it would happen, and it did.'

"Now, if it hadn't worked for us in the Maryland game, it would have worked eventually. It would have just taken a little longer, that's all."

Was there some luck involved?

Nehlen said, "I don't know. How do you know that? The kids had worked their tails off. All I know is, that day in College Park we were a team equal to Maryland. The year before we weren't. This time we were in a position to take advantage of one bounce of the ball. It came our way and we capitalized on it. If the bounce had gone the other way, they would have won. That's usually what close games are all about. It's just that our new attitude toward strength to put us in a position to win, and we did."

After that, the Mountaineers worked harder in the weight room. The coach sensed a different air about them. "I swear," he said, "they walked differently down the hall. They knew they had beaten a big-time team, a team that went to a bowl the season before. And they did it away from home.

"Daggone, we were 2-0 and had it going."

Despite the great start, turmoil continued to swirl around the Mountaineer athletic program. That spring, Athletic Director Dick Martin, the man who hired Nehlen, resigned after a $650,000 error was discovered in the 1980-81 athletic budget. A few months later, Fred Schaus, former WVU basketball great and basketball coach of the Mountaineers and Los Angeles Lakers, was hired to succeed Martin. The WVU administration hoped Schaus, who had the reputation of being "frugal,' could straighten it out. But for the present, the athletic department had a monstrous cash flow problem.

Nehlen and his emerging "giant" of a program would eventually take care of that problem.

Meanwhile, the appearance of the Mountaineers in the football polls failed to impress Nehlen. He insisted polls didn't mean a thing until the final one of the season.

Besides, he was too busy trying to improve his team in the areas where he knew it was weak.

The unbeaten Mountaineers returned home after the Maryland win and played Colorado State. They were favored for the first time in the season — by 14 points. A crowd of 48,714 turned out and watched the team romp to its third straight win, 49-3. WVU, despite the win, for some reason dropped out of the polls. It was suspected that Colorado State Coach Sark Arslanian, who was on the UPI coaches' poll committee, voted the Mountaineers way up in the polls the week before so he and his team wouldn't look bad when they lost.

Anyhow, WVU was off to its best start since the 1975 Peach Bowl team.

Nehlen praised the play of quarterback Luck, who completed 16 of 22 passes for 198 yards and four touchdowns against Colorado State. "He's like the interest rates," he said. "He's money in the bank."

Nehlen called the Colorado State win "about as big as the one at Maryland."

He explained, "If you remember, before I came to West Virginia, Colorado State had beaten West Virginia, 50-14. They really embarrassed the team. Then, my first year we went out there and turned the tables, 52-24. Then, they came to our place and we handed them a worse beating. If you're a smart coach, you can use that kind of stuff to work on your players' heads. I think I'm fairly smart.

"I told the team, 'You see, men, what's happened here in the last year with our strength program, our confidence, all our sticking together and having no one care who gets the credit? We played a team like Colorado State, which two years embarrassed us and our program, and we totally dominated them.'

"You have to have something your players can believe in. And they certainly could believe in that."

Nehlen beamed about the team's turnover ratio. In three games the Mountaineers had run 237 plays and committed two turnovers (no fumbles and two interceptions). That was one every 118.5 plays. "When you play mistake-free football, you can win," he said. "When you make mistakes, you lose."

Nehlen's philosophy about turnovers was to always remain positive when a player fumbled, dropped a pass, jumped offsides or threw an interception.

"You're better than that," he would say. "Don't worry about it." And then he always gave the player a fatherly pat on the rump.

West Virginia was winning, but the injury list continued to grow. Defensive captain Calvin Turner was sidelined with a bruised knee and would miss the road trip to ever-dangerous Boston College.

Nehlen moaned, "We're into the meat of our schedule. If the injuries continue, we won't have enough players left to play the weak sisters of the poor."

In an attempt to fill the gaps on his traveling squad, he took 13 freshmen to Chestnut Hill, Mass.

"We're not taking those young pups to Boston just to feed them and put them up one night in a hotel," he said.

"Some of them will have to play."

Nehlen didn't need any of them, because his defense intercepted four passes and the offense rolled to a 17-3 halftime lead and won handily, 38-10. Boston College crossed midfield only once the second half, and that came on a roughing-the-kicker penalty against the Mountaineers. And Boston College's only touchdown came with 30 seconds to play when it blocked a punt by a second-string freshman punter named Paul Woodside.

Nehlen fumed about that. "We gave up a TD on a stupid mistake," he snapped. "We let down. If we make a mistake like that in a close game, it'll beat us." He was angry about something else, too — about a picture on the cover of the Boston College-West Virginia game program that depicted a raggedy hillbilly running from a dilapidated shack.

He said, "That's an insult to our state, our school and our program. We are not hillbillies. We're Mountaineers. And I'm sick of this kind of bull crap."

Regardless, West Virginia was now 4-0 and had won three of them on the road. The team was 15th in the nation in total defense, and although not rated in the wire service polls, it was 19th in a poll by Football News. However, the Pitt Panthers were next on the schedule. They were No. 1 in total defense and rated No. 4 in everybody's poll.

In three games, the Panthers had held opponents to minus 10 yards rushing.

An all-time record crowd of 54,280 turned out at Mountaineer Field on October 10 to see the struggle. After a scoreless first quarter, the Mountaineers began to drive from the Pitt 46. Eight plays later, they were at the Pitt 15. Second down and one. Tailback Curlin Beck took a handoff and broke clear. He was hit at the one and fumbled. Pitt recovered in the endzone.

Touchback. Pitt's ball at its own 20.

Then, with 1:57 to play in the half, Pitt scored on a 43-yard run by Bryan Thomas to take a 7-0 halftime lead. Nehlen mumbled, "If only Beck hadn't fumbled going into the endzone . . ."

Pitt scored 10 more points in the second half and won, 17-0. West Virginia was limited to only 60 yards rushing and 92 passing, and Luck completed just 16 of 36 passes and had three intercepted. The Mountaineers also lost that one fumble by Beck.

"What did I tell you about turnovers?" Nehlen said afterward. "In a tight game they'll kill you. You can't turn the ball over to a good team and expect to win. And if someone knows how to run the ball against Pitt, I wish he'd write me a letter.

Pitt Coach Jackie Sherrill wasn't as critical of West Virginia as Nehlen. He said, "West Virginia is a much-improved football team. I'm not surprised. I knew when they hired Don Nehlen, they were getting a fine coach. They'll get better, too."

People were beginning to notice Nehlen and the Mountaineers. West Virginia hadn't had a game televised in five years. The Pitt game wasn't on TV, either. But ABC-TV sent a crew to Mountainer Field and filmed highlights of the game to show during the telecast of its regularly scheduled game. Also, a few days earlier the TV crew filmed Nehlen and Oliver Luck and aired the film on its "Flashback" feature at halftime of the next week's "NCAA College Football" game.

The homecoming game the next week was against Virginia Tech, a team that had humiliated the Mountaineers, 34-11, the year before. Nehlen expressed deep concern about it, because the Monday before the game 22 of his players were on the sidelines and couldn't practice. Luck had a severely sprained ankle and was on crutches. "I don't know if Luck will be able to play," said Nehlen. "He certainly can't practice."

Luck played. Did he ever! He completed 17 of 27 passes for 265 yards and three touchdowns as the Mountaineers rolled up 436 yards total offense. Rich Hollins caught two of them for touchdowns of 73 and two yards. West Virginia's defense, now No. 4 in the nation, held Tech to 131 yards total offense and the Mountaineers won, 27-6.

They were now 5-1 and a trip to the base of Mount Nittany to battle Penn State was next. The Nittany Lions were undefeated and No. 1 in the polls. Nehlen knew his team was in for a long afternoon. "We've got only three healthy defensive tackles," he moaned. "I'm going to have to take some tackles from our scout team up there, and hope I don't have to use them."

It didn't matter. A record Beaver Stadium crowd of 85,017 turned out to watch Penn State extend its domination over the Mountaineers to 23 consecutive games with a 30-7 victory. Luck threw 37 passes and connected on 24 for 226 yards, but couldn't match the Lions crunching ground attack (341 yards) and Todd Blackledge's 9-for-15 passing.

Hostetler, the kid who backed up Blackledge at quarterback for Penn State the year before, no longer wore the blue and white of the Lions. He transferred to West Virginia, was sitting out the season and would be eligible in 1982.

After the game, Penn State Coach Joe Paterno said, "Obviously, West Virginia is a much better team. It is the best West Virginia team I've seen in a long, long time and the best team we've played to date this year. I honestly believe West Virginia's front-line people are comparable to Nebraska's." Earlier in the season, Penn State had played at Nebraska and won, 30-24.

About 15 minutes after the Penn State loss, Nehlen stood in a corner of the locker room awaiting questions from sportswriters. One of the first questions asked was by a writer from Philadelphia. He asked, "Did you have a game plan, coach?"

Nehlen stared at the guy as if he hadn't heard the question right. He answered, "What did you say? Did we have a game plan?

"No, we didn't have a game plan. We just came up here and fooled around. Hell, yes, we had a game plan. Unfortunately, it didn't work. What kind of a question is that? What do you think we are, dumb or something? We played a superior team and got beat, that's all. A lot of teams come in here with game plans that don't work.

"Did we have a game plan? Of all the stupid questions

I've ever heard, that takes the cake."

Game plan or not, the Mountaineers were now 5-2. But guess what? Scouts from the Tangerine, Peach, Hall of Fame and Garden State bowls were at the Penn State game. They weren't there to scout the No. 1 team in the nation. Major bowls are the ones that do that.

The following week WVU got "feelers" from three bowls. The Tangerine Bowl let Fred Schaus know "they were interested." The Peach Bowl called to say, "We like your team, and love your fans." The Garden State Bowl invited Nehlen to attend its weekly press conference at the Meadowlands in New Jersey.

Nehlen said, "I'm not concerned about bowls at this time. We need to win three more games to be a true bowl contender. But the interest from the bowls proves one thing — Penn State is not the key to our season. These next games are the keys to our season.

"I'm just afraid all this bowl talk will put pressure on the players. They're not mature enough yet to handle that kind of pressure. Good programs can handle it, but we're not there yet. We can't afford to look ahead and listen to bowl talk. That would be fatal."

West Virginia was favored over its next two opponents and responded by beating East Carolina, 20-3, and Temple, 24-19. The record stood at 7-2 (only three other major independent teams could match that) and Nehlen was assured of his first winning season at WVU. For the fourth straight week scouts from the Tangerine Bowl scouted the Mountaineers. The Peach, Hall of Fame and Garden State bowls were still interested. The Liberty and Independence Bowl started scouting WVU, too. And Schaus said the Sun Bowl had also expressed interest.

Although Nehlen insisted he wasn't thinking about bowls, he admitted his team was. "The players know what's at stake," he said. "They aren't stupid."

Prior to the Temple game, Nehlen didn't have time to think about bowls. He had to find another field goal kicker. Murat Tercan, the regular kicker, was jogging around Mountaineer Field, and tripped, fell down and injured his knee. Nehlen said, "I can't believe it. What's going to happen next?"

What happened next was Nehlen promoted freshman Woodside, the walk-on from Falls Church, Va., who had the punt blocked earlier against Boston College, to No. 1. Woodside booted a 25-yard field goal and was 3 for 3 in extra points against Temple. It was a promotion that would have a bearing on changing the image of WVU football.

Rutgers was next. A crowd of 44,935 turned out for the final home game at Mountaineer Field. That crowd brought WVU's average attendance for the year to a record 44,145.

Bowl scouts were in the Mountaineer Field press box and saw the Mountaineers plod to a lackluster 20-3 victory. But it was a victory. The record was now 8-2.

Nehlen said, "Yes, we've talked about bowls. It's difficult to hide something like that when you're 8-2. Our kids know that teams with eight wins usually go to bowls."

He added, "When I took this job I told my wife

(Merry Ann), that I was going into a losing program and that it would probably take three or four years to get it going — even if we had a little luck. I told her to hang onto her hat because things could get rough before they got better. And here we are, 8-2 and heading into our last game of our second season. Did I foresee this happening so soon? No, not really. Prior to the season, I looked at the schedule and tried to figure out how we'd win six games. It's just a tremendous tribute to the hard work, dedication and sacrifice of our players.

"I've been asked if I thought we'd be a bowl contender this year. Are you kidding? No way. Sure, we've had some luck, but we've been well-prepared, too. We are developing a winning attitude.

"When I took this job, there were some players who didn't want to conform to my way of thinking. They are gone, because I sure wouldn't conform to them. The kids I have now want to get stronger. We are stronger. Now, the players on opposing teams try to block my kids, they bounce off. We aren't strong enough yet, but we're heading in the right direction."

The next day, November 15, it was unofficial, but the word leaked out — Nehlen's Mountaineers had a bid to the December 31 Peach Bowl in Atlanta and would play the winner of the November 28 Florida-Florida State game. Of course, bowl bids couldn't officially be extended until after the final games the upcoming Saturday.

West Virginia had to travel to the new Syracuse Carrier Dome and play the Syracuse Orangemen that day. And one thing was official, the TV network had finally taken notice of the Mountaineers and was going to regionally televise the game. It was West Virginia's first TV appearance since the Pitt game in 1976.

The word was that WVU would receive the bid to the Peach Bowl regardless of whether or not it beat Syracuse. Bowl or no bowl, Nehlen wanted to win this one, because it would give the team nine wins, something only two other teams in WVU history had been able to do. Also, the Mountaineers were back in the polls, rated No. 19 by United Press International. He wanted his team to stay in the polls.

"We have a chance for a 9-2 season," he said. "I think the team will play with great emotion against Syracuse. We have so many of our pre-season goals within our reach. We'd better play with great emotion, because as far as I'm concerned Syracuse is better than the last three teams we've played."

Also, Nehlen was worried that all the bowl talk had taken his players' mind off the game.

"In our Sunday night meeting before the Syracuse game," Nehlen said, "none of my players wanted to talk about Syracuse. All they wanted to know was, 'Which bowl are we going to?' Now, I know that's normal, but it sure makes game preparation tough.

"And my coaches were the same. They were saying, 'I wonder where we are going and who we'll play? All of a sudden, the game at Syracuse seemed unimportant. But I knew it wasn't.

"Even Fred Schaus was calling me every so often and saying, 'Right now, it looks like the Peach Bowl.'

"Then he'd call later and say, 'It looks like we'll play the Florida-Florida State winner. When I find out, I'll call you back.'

"In the meantime, I was trying to get my team ready for a tough game. The entire week before the Syracuse game was tough. There seemed to be absolutely no concentration, no intensity, nothing . . . nothing but bowl talk."

In the first 30 minutes against Syracuse, he was pleasantly surprised. His Mountaineers played near-perfect football. They jumped off to a 17-7 lead. Quarterback Luck completed 18 of 22 passes for 178 yards and a touchdown. And tailback Mickey Walczak rushed eight times for 38 yards. The offense gained 243 yards in the first half.

"It looked like a rout," said Nehlen. "Then, when I went into the locker room at halftime, I sensed something was wrong.

"I could tell right then and there that something was wrong with my football team. We had a good lead, but things were going too easy for us. The players felt they had the game won. I knew they didn't. I knew Dick McPherson (Syracuse coach) was a fighter. I knew his kids would come back fighting in the second half.

"I told my kids, 'Hey, I sensed a loss of concentration near the end of the half. Concentrate! If you do that, and execute, we ought to be able to run our plays like stealing candy from a baby. And you linemen, I want you to slug a few guys — legally, of course. Pop! You know what I mean.'

"But I told Gary (offensive coordinator Gary Tranquill), 'Gary, we have a problem.'

"He said, 'What problem? What the heck are you talking about?'

"I said, 'Gary, I'm telling you we've lost this football game. Our kids are glassy-eyed. There is no emotion, no spark. They think with a 17-7 lead they have the game won.'

"Gary said, 'Don't worry, Don. Syracuse can't beat us.'

"I hate to admit it, but I was right. I wish I had been wrong. In the second half, I said to myself, 'Whose team is that on the field? It certainly isn't mine.' We went tentative and if I had an explanation for it, I'd market it and make a fortune."

Syracuse, paced by running back Joe Morris, came out in the final 30 minutes, scored 20 points and beat the Mountaineers, 27-24.

That defeat made many of the WVU brass nervous, because Peach Bowl scout Art Gregory was in the press box and witnessed the defeat. Afterward, he immediately placed a call from the press box to bowl headquarters in Atlanta. A rumor had circulated that if the Mountaineers lost, the Peach Bowl might take South Carolina, if it beat Clemson. Perhaps Gregory and the bowl committee were waiting for the results of the South Carolina-Clemson game. (Clemson beat South Carolina, 29-13).

Down in the WVU locker room, the Mountaineers and Nehlen were waiting for Gregory to show up and officially extend them the bowl bid. Although Nehlen was convinced the Mountaineers had the bid regardless, he was still nervous. Bowl committees have been known to change their minds at the 11th hour.

"I thought maybe they were backing out after the way we stunk up the place in the second half," Nehlen said.

The minutes went by and no Gregory. He was still on the phone in the press box. WVU Athletic Director Fred Schaus feared the bowl committee might have had a change of heart. "Where is he?" Schaus asked, scanning the empty stands. Schaus sent assistant sports information Tim Lilly off to find Gregory. "Maybe he can't find his way to the locker room," Schaus said, to no one in particular.

After what seemed an eternity, sports information director Mike Parsons said, "Here he comes."

Sure enough, it was Gregory sprinting across the artificial turf toward the WVU locker room.

Was there a problem?

Gregory said, "No. Just a mixup in communications. I was on the phone just to give the committee an update on the outcome of the game. There was never any doubt about inviting West Virginia. In fact, West Virginia was a unanimous selection of the committee.

"Naturally, we would have preferred that West Virginia win this game. But a three-point defeat to a good Syracuse team on Syracuse's home indoor field, where noise is a big factor, is no disgrace."

And then he turned to the Mountaineers and said, "On behalf of the Peach Bowl committee, I want to extend you an invitation to play in the Peach Bowl in Atlanta, Ga., on December 31 against the winner of the Florida-Florida State game."

The Mountaineers cheered. They knew it was WVU's first bowl bid in six years. Schaus was relieved, because he could now start selling the 15,000 Peach Bowl tickets the bowl had sent him during the week.

"See," laughed Nehlen, "We had the bid all along. There really wasn't any suspense."

And on November 28, the Florida Gators defeated former WVU Coach Bobby Bowden Florida State Seminoles, 35-3.

50

Chapter Ten

An Orlando Sentinel sports columnist wrote of the West Virginia-Florida matchup in the 1981 Peach Bowl: "West Virginia trying to play Florida will be like the Afghanistans trying to fend off the Russians."

The writer suggested that Eastern football was rinky-dink compared to the great brand of football played in the Southeastern Conference, a conference Florida was a member of. He not only questioned West Virginia's credentials to play in the bowl but also implied the Mountaineers had no business in it at all.

Don Nehlen said he "was amused" by the column. That's what he said. But what he did was use it as a psychologist's weapon to arouse his team. However, it's doubtful the Mountaineers needed any arousing after the way Nehlen had prepared them.

"The columnist took the usual shot people always take at us," Nehlen said, "about our hillbilly image. It was just something else I could use to help get my team ready to play.

"We weren't as good as Florida, but my kids didn't know that. And I wasn't going to let them know it."

National betting services apparently agreed with the Orlando columnist's evaluation of the Mountaineers, because the day before the game the national betting line favored Florida by 13 1/2 points. Some oddmakers even had Florida favored by 17 points. A bet on the Gators to win was called "the lock of the year."

In Las Vegas, so much money was bet on Florida that the game was taken off the board.

Nehlen said, "I heard about that Orlando newspaper column when one of our fans called from Florida and read it to me over the phone. Then a fan gave me a copy of it. All I did was put it on the bulletin board in our locker room.

"If that columnist, and Florida, wanted to badmouth us, that was fine. The people who count know all about the quality of Eastern football.

"That Orlando writer wrote, too, about us playing only a two-game schedule, Pitt and Penn State, and losing both. And Florida people figured because of our 'poor' schedule, we didn't have a prayer. We were kind of anxious to play the football game."

The 8-3 Mountaineers weren't a rinky-dink team. Three weeks before the bowl game, two of the Mountaineers' linebackers (outside linebacker Darryl Talley and tight end Mark Raugh) had been named third team All-Americans by the Associated Press. Quarterback Oliver Luck, defensive tackle Todd Campbell and defensive back Lind Murray were on the honorable mention list. United Press International had the Mountaineers No. 19 in its poll. The committee of the North-South All-Star game in Mobile, Ala., thought enough of Nehlen's coaching that it asked him to coach the North team. Nehlen had to decline when WVU got the bowl bid.

Florida was paced by sophomore quarterback Wayne Peace. He had a bevy of swift, talented receivers. And on defense, the Gators were led by a 283-pound tackle named David Galloway, who would be a first-round NFL draft pick.

The 7-4 Gators had beaten Florida State (35-3), Louisiana State (24-10), Maryland (15-10), Ole Miss (49-3), Kentucky (33-12), Georgia Tech (27-6) and Furman (35-7). Their losses had been to Miami (21-20), Mississippi State (28-7), Auburn (14-12), and Georgia and ace Herchel Walker (26-21).

Prior to the game, Nehlen said, ". Florida has a fine quarterback. And they are like us, they like to throw the ball. I would say Florida is better than Pitt and Penn State because they have more speed and their kicking game is better. Florida is for real."

Nehlen had known Florida was for real for weeks. He had studied films of the Gators' games by the hour in an effort to find some weaknesses in their offense and defense.

"As I looked at the films," he said, "I was about ready to agree with the experts. Maybe we didn't belong on the field with them. Listen, Florida was one fine team. It had the quickest defense we had seen all year. Those guys simply ran everybody down. I mean, they had speed to burn."

So, Nehlen reasoned, "Why not use Florida's speed to our advantage?"

And he and offensive coordinator Gary Tranquill put their heads together and added three "little wrinkles" to their offense.

"We put in a cutback, or counter, to the fullback, a fullback draw and a quarterback draw," said Nehlen. "We figured Florida's linebackers would pursue like crazy. And if we could get them over-committing, we could use their speed to work against them. We had run a halfback draw during the season, but never a fullback draw. And we had Ollie (Luck) sprinting out. We knew as soon as they saw Ollie sprinting out, their linebackers would start running to head him off.

"All we did was have Ollie drop the ball off to fullback Dane Conwell."

On defense, Nehlen took a big gamble. The Gators' films showed that quarterback Peace did a lot of sprinting out — right and left. The films showed, too, that Peace wasn't a speed-burner. "That's when we decided to go with nickel defense," Nehlen said. "Five defensive backs. We gambled that Florida would come out throwing the ball, and we were determined to put pressure on their quarterback.

"We had them framed up. On every play we were going to have that fifth defensive back blitzing. And they had nobody to block him unless they changed their entire defensive scheme. We didn't think they could do that."

Nehlen's plan involved a guessing game, because if he blitzed his fifth defensive back from the right and Florida's quarteback sprinted to the left, or vice-versa, it could be costly. Also, the Mountaineers' defensive alignment left them vulnerable to the run.

"The worst thing we could do was guess wrong," he said. "But even if we guessed wrong, we felt they couldn't block our blitzer, and he could still put heat on their passer."

After deciding what he was going to use to attack Florida, Nehlen began to work on his players' heads.

"You have to understand," he said, "when you are going to play a team that is clearly better than you are, and you have four weeks to prepare, you have to do more than get your team ready physically. You have to get them ready mentally — individually and collectively. So, we challenged them every day."

Nehlen explained that offensive tackle Keith Jones was one he especially singled out, because Jones would be assigned the task of blocking Florida's giant tackle, David Galloway.

"Our kids had read in the papers every day about how much better Florida was than they were, "Nehlen said. "Writers said our kids were no good, that they couldn't compete, that they had no business going against a team like Florida.

"I remember challenging Jones about playing opposite Galloway. I challenged him in front of the team. I told him, 'Keith, why don't you quit? Nobody will ever know. You're a senior. You've had a good career. You don't have to go the Peach Bowl and let Galloway embarrass you.'

"Then, sometimes during practice, one of the players would say to Jones, 'Keith, you are still out here? We thought you quit.'

"And by the time the game rolled around, Keith Jones was ready to eat nickels."

It was cloudy and cold (34 degrees) on Dec. 31 in Atlanta, Ga. It rained that morning, but stopped about two hours before the kickoff. Florida won the toss and elected to receive. Freshman Paul Woodside moved forward and booted the ball. And 37,582 fans and a nationwide television audience settled back to watch the carnage.

In three plays, the Gators gained nine yards and punted. The Mountaineers had the ball on their own 23. Two plays netted one yard. But on a third-and-nine situation, Luck went up the middle on that quarterback draw

play for 12 yards and a first down.

The public address announcer said into the mike, "Virginia's ball."

Nehlen glanced angrily in the direction of the press box. "Jesus criminy, it's WEST VIRGINIA!" he muttered to himself.

Then, Luck rolled out and passed for eight yards to tailback Mickey Walczak. Next, it was fullback Conwell for six on that counter play. First down.

Luck completed consecutive passes for six yards to Raugh and 13 yards to Rich Hollins. WVU had a first down at the Florida 31. After an outside penalty against the Gators, Luck hit Walczak for 11 yards and another first down, and handed off to Conwell on the fullback draw for eight more yards.

And on second down and two at the Florida seven-yard line, Luck rolled right and hit Walczak in the corner of the end zone for a touchdown. Woodside kicked the extra point and WVU led, 7-0. It had taken the Mountaineers five minutes to score.

On Florida's second possession, quarterback Peace had his second pass batted down by the WVU rush. His third pass was intercepted by Lind Murray. Nehlen's plan to go with five defensive backs and "put heat on" the passer seemed to be working.

In the first half, Mountaineer cornerback Donnie Stemple, that fifthback, came up with three tackles for losses. Plus, he batted down one pass. "I was breathing down the back of Peace's helmet on almost every play," said Stemple, a senior second-string walk-on who was making his first and only start as a Mountaineer.

Woodside kicked field goals of 35, 42, and 49 yards (the 49-yarder was a Peach Bowl record), and West Virginia led at the half, 16-10. Florida, mainly because of Stemple's quarterback sacks, had minus 12 yards rushing and only 39 yards passing.

"We were afraid at the half that Florida might switch to a running game, because that's where we were weak," said Nehlen. "But they didn't. So, we stayed with our nickel defense."

In the second half, Stemple blitzed and blitzed from the outside. Because of the pressure, Peace fumbled, was tackled for lost yardage, threw another interception and ended the game with six completions in 13 attempts for just 47 yards. Also, because of the pressure, the Gators suffered 86 yards in losses.

Stemple was voted the game's outstanding defensive player.

On offense, the Mountaineers, led by Luck's passing and the running of Conwell, scored more points and led, 26-0, going into the game's final minutes. Luck completed 14 of 23 passes for 107 yards and one touchdown, and rushed nine times for 25 yards.

Conwell (or Cornwall, as the official statistician called him) had the biggest game of his career as he rushed for 97 yards on 26 carries.

Florida got on the scoreboard with 3:03 to play with a touchdown against the Mountaineer's second-team defense.

Final score was: West Virginia 26, Florida 6.

Afterward, Nehlen said, "We proved today we can play. I'm proud of everybody. This victory is a big plus for our program. I kinda think Florida took us too lightly. Our kids just went out and kicked their rumps.

"Some wise guy asked me if that column that writer wrote in the Orlando newspaper had anything to do with our win. That's so ridiculous, it's not even worth commenting on. I guarantee you it took a lot more than some guy saying we weren't very good in a newspaper article in order for us to win.

"But the writer just reinforced what I had been telling our players — that they weren't respected. It's a funny thing about the word 'respect.' When kids feel they aren't respected as football players, they can get pretty excited about playing.

"We won because we didn't give their quarterback a chance to catch his breath all day. Stemple was either in his face, or breathing down his neck every time he touched the ball. And let me tell you, as a former quarterback, I know you can feel it when a guy is bearing down on you from behind. You may not see him, but you can sure feel him. That'll rattle a quarterback quicker than anything else.

"Our offensive line did a great job, particularly Keith Jones, of protecting Ollie Luck. Jones didn't let Florida's big Galloway kid get to Luck all day.

"And how about our field kicker? My man Woody (Paul Woodside) kicked four field goals, including that 49-yarder for a Peach Bowl record. The kid is a walk-on and not a scholarship. It looks like he'll get one now.

"And you want to know something else? We should have shut Florida out. They didn't score until we put in the second team late in the game. I wanted to give some of your younger players a chance to play. They needed the experience. And besides, I think every kid should have a chance to play in a bowl game. Denny (defensive cooridinator Dennis Brown) was mad, though. He wanted his defense to get a shutout."

Mountaineer fans came up with a new phrase — "How about them Eers?"

West Virginia ended the season 9-3, only the third time in history that a Mountaineer team finished with nine wins. And in the final wire service polls, Nehlen's team was voted 17th by the Associated Press and 18th by United Press International. The Mountaineers had made the top 20 in the "poll that counted." The final one.

It's a tribute to the hard work, sacrifice and dedication of the players," Nehlen said. "Also, my coaches did a tremendous job of getting the team ready to play.

The approximately 20,000 West Virginia fans were in seventh heaven. Some were worried, too, because they know that the last two times the Mountaineers won Peach Bowl games that they lost their head coaches. Jim Carlen left for Texas Tech after the 14-3 win over South Carolina in 1969, and Bobby Bowden went to Florida State after the 13-10 win over North Carolina State in 1975.

Their worries were justified, because in less than a week it was reported that Nehlen had been offered the head coaching position at South Carolina. He drove to Charleston, West Virginia and discussed the job with South Carolina athletic director Bob Marcum, who two years earlier recommended Nehlen for the WVU job.

Nehlen said, "South Carolina offered me a $131,000-a-year package, and that didn't include any money from speeches. That was just base salary and a radio and TV show. At the time I was making $48,000 at West Virginia. I could almost triple my salary, and get a five-year contract. (Nehlen had a four-year pact at WVU.)

"Marcum wanted me to fly down to Columbia on a Wednesday and sign the contract. Was I interested in the job? Sure, I was interested."

Marcum admitted he tried to hire Nehlin and said, "I took some criticism when the news leaked out.

Nehlen said, "I just felt it was wrong for several reasons. Although I could have taken all my coaches to South Carolina, I was advised that it would be best to hire some coaches who were familiar with the area. So, that meant I could take only half my staff. How was I going to call my coaches together and tell half of them that 'It was nice, but I'll see you later?' No way. I don't operate like that.

"When I took the job at West Virginia, I told Dick Martin I wouldn't be walking out. There was nothing in writing, but I had given my word and that meant something to me. I told him, 'I don't plan on going anywhere.'

"Also, my players weren't in school at the time. They were home, still on the holiday break. I couldn't walk out on them.

"I'm not naive enough to think we were 9-3 and I was offered the South Carolina job because of Don Nehlen. It all came about because of my staff, my players, my equipment man, my trainers. All of us. I was just one person in the total program.

"I'm no more deserving when we win than all those other guys. And I might add I'm no more at fault when we lose than those other guys. But I knew I couldn't leave any of my people behind. I couldn't do that.

"I finally sat down with Mac (wife Merry Ann) and said, 'What do you want to do?.'

"She said, I love West Virginia. I want to stay.'

"After that, we went for a drive, and when we got home there was a big crowd outside the house. I thought maybe there had been a fire or something. Here it was people from Morgantown who had come to the house to show us what they thought of us. They were chanting, 'Don, don't go . . . Don, don't go.

"I couldn't believe it."

A few hours after that, Don Nehlen called Marcum and told him he was going to remain at West Virginia. "It was an awful lot of money to turn down," Nehlen said. "But I told Marcum that the whole thing bothered me. You have to understand, Marcum was a friend of mine and I didn't want to hurt him.

"Marcum said, 'What's bothering you, Don?

"I said, 'The whole thing. The timing. I don't know. I just don't feel good about it. I thought I would be elated, but I'm not. You don't want a coach coming to a job who feels that way. And I don't want to come feeling that way.'

"I've always been a guy who does things on gut feelings. The feeling wasn't there.

"Before I made my decision to turn down the South Carolina offer, I remember walking through our new weight room in the facilities building. I looked at all the things I wanted to do in that room. And I said, 'This room isn't the way I want it. And here I am thinking about leaving this place?

"Hell, I haven't even begun.'

Chapter Eleven

It was bedlam in the West Virginia University locker room underneath the end zone stands in Atlanta's Fulton County Stadium. The Mountaineers were celebrating, and for good reason. They had just humiliated the Florida Gators, 26-6, in the 1981 Peach Bowl.

It was a game no one, except a few die-hard Mountaineer fans, figured West Virginia would win.

Don Nehlen gathered his squad around him and said, "Men, you are dynamite. Just dynamite. You dominated a good football team today. And you did it on national television.

"Now, bring on Oklahoma!"

The Mountaineers, who finished the season with a bowl victory, a 9-3 record and a position in the nation's final top 20 polls, were scheduled to open 1982 campaign at Norman, Okla., against the mighty Oklahoma Sooners.

Oklahoma! The team famed for its wishbone and hurry-up offense. The team that romped and stomped over opponents with its blinding speed. The team that was always among the rushing leaders. The team that had averaged 10 wins a year during the previous six seasons. The team that was one of the darlings of television. The team that annually was up in the polls and went to bowls. The team that had won several national championships.

Nehlen added, "Now, next September we have to do what no West Virginia team has ever done. We have to go to Oklahoma — and win! And that's what we're going to do."

Nehlen had done his homework about WVU and Oklahoma. He knew the Mountaineers, under former coach Frank Cignetti, had gone to Norman in 1978 and had been humiliated, 52-10.

He knew all about the Oklahoma horse and covered wagon. He knew it was a tradition at Oklahoma that every time the Sooners score a touchdown, a small horse, pulling a wagon, comes out of the Memorial Stadium tunnel and gallops around the field. Sooner fans, all wearing red and waving red pennants and pom-poms, go wild.

"The last time a West Virginia team played at Oklahoma, it darned near ran that Sooners' horse to death," Nehlen mused. "I didn't plan on taking my team out there and killing that horse. We planned on giving it lots of rest.

"In that 1978 game, Oklahoma's starters didn't even wear their shoulder pads the second half. They were on the sidelines and spent the whole half signing autographs and shaking hands with fans. No sir, I didn't plan on taking a team out there and getting beat by 50 points."

He knew that Oklahoma lost home openers about once every two decades. Last opening defeat for the Sooners was 1960.

Nehlen knew, too, that the Peach Bowl victory had moved his Mountaineers up a rung on the college football prestige ladder, but that they were still "one rung" from the top. Although his team had been rated in the 20 after the Florida victory, Nehlen felt that WVU was really only "a top 30 team" at best and still had a way to go in the building process.

The '82 opener was reminiscent of the tough openers Nehlen had when he coached at Bowling Green, where he earned the title of 'Master of the Upset' with wins over Purdue and Syracuse. "We had eight months to prepare for this one, "and by jiminy, we were going to do it."

The first thing Nehlen did upon returning to Morgantown from the Peach Bowl was have his team out to his house, and wife Merry Ann fed them. Merry Ann has always fed her husband's teams.

Nehlen recalled, "We were sitting around the house and a couple of fifth-year seniors who had played on the team that lost at Oklahoma in '78 said, 'Coach, you wouldn't believe it! There we were out there dying in that Oklahoma heat — must have been 120 degrees on the AstroTurf — and getting killed. Every time they scored that horse came running out of the tunnel. And their guys were over by the stands signing autographs. They really humiliated us.'

"I told them, 'I don't know if we're going to beat Oklahoma, but I can guarantee you one thing, that horse is going to get a day off. Somehow, we're going to make Oklahoma pass the football. We're going to stop their running game. If they beat us, they're going to have to do it passing the ball.

"And they don't know how.'

"Now, for us to have a chance, I told the players they had to get busy in the weight room. They had gotten stronger the winter before, but weren't stong enough yet — not for the schedule we had facing us in '82."

And Nehlen began studying as many films on Oklahoma as he could get his hands on. He called coaches in the Big Eight Conference whose teams played the Sooners every year and pumped them for information. "When you have had success against Oklahoma, what did you do?" he asked. Nehlen was trying to find a chink in Oklahoma's offensive armor. What he found out in talking to coaches at Nebraska, Oklahoma State, Texas, etc., was that his Mountaineers weren't going to stop the

Sooners' awesome wishbone with their regular defense.

Nehlen said, "We were told, if we did that, they'd pick us to death. But I had already figured that out."

The next thing Nehlen did was get with his staff and dissect the blocking scheme of the Oklahoma wishbone. The Sooners put three backs in the backfield and a guard, tackle and end on either side of the ball.

West Virginia's regular defense had a linebacker, tackle, end and a cornerback on either side of the ball.

"That meant Oklahoma would have six people to our four," Nehlen said, "Oh, we might get five to the play if one of our other guys ran to the ball. But we'd still be outmanned. We couldn't stop the wishbone with a regular defense. We had to come up with something else."

The defense Nehlen came up with was another big gamble, like the nickel defense he had successfully used against Florida in the Peach Bowl. "We had to find a way to get five guys lined up on either side of the ball and a guy in the middle to key on the quarterback," he said. "So, we decided to bring free safety Tim Agee up in the middle. Agee was to key on the fullback and go with the flow. Now, sometimes he would take the quarterback, and sometimes he would take the pitch man. We just sorta mixed it up.

"But we were taking a tremendous gamble. When you have that many people up to play the run, you are giving up a heckuva lot in the secondary. We decided to dare them to throw. And we were sure they wouldn't, because they prided themselves so much on their ability to run the ball."

Offensively, Nehlen had a bigger gamble facing him. Oliver Luck, the straight-A Rhodes Scholarship candidate who broke nearly every school passing record, was gone. Replacing him would be Jeff Hostetler, the junior transfer from Penn State. Nehlen had no doubts about Hostetler's ability. But debuting against Oklahoma was a tall order for the young man from Hollsopple, Pa.

Prior to the start of pre-season practice, the Mountaineers got an unexpected shot of confidence. In one football magazine, Florida, the team they had humiliated in the Peach Bowl, was picked as the choice to finish No. 1 that year. "You could see our players react to that," Nehlen said. They thought, 'If the experts think Florida is going to be that good, then we must be pretty good, too.' "

At media day on Aug. 15, Nehlen stood on the turf at Mountaineer Field and talked to writers about the Sept. 11 opener against the Sooners. He said, "You guys all want to know how we're going to do when we open against Oklahoma. I don't know. Only the good Lord knows the answer to that. But I know one thing, we're not going to be intimidated. Our guys have worked like crazy in the weight room in the off-season. They are beginning to believe that with strength they have a chance to win.

"I'll bet many of you were surprised when we beat Florida in the Peach Bowl. We weren't. We believed we could win.

"Now, Oklahoma, well, that's a different story. I'm anxious to play those guys. I don't know exactly what we'll do, because I'm not that smart. But I do know when we

play the Sooners and have a third-down-and-11, they aren't going to know what we're going to do, either,"

Nehlen made it sound good. But the truth was he knew exactly what he was going to do. The Mountaineers were going to throw the ball, and throw and throw. And if that didn't work, they were going to throw some more, because Nehlen was convinced Oklahoma didn't know how to defend against his team's sophisticated passing attack.

The next thing he did was begin his 'psychology game.'

The report from the Oklahoma prairie-country was that the Sooners were practicing in 100-degree heat, and the temperature on the turf in Oklahoma'a stadium was "almost 120 degrees." West Virginia was about to begin practice in Morgantown where the weather for that mid-August was unusually cool.

"Great weather for golf, but not for getting a team ready to play in the Oklahoma heat," moaned the WVU coach privately. "The heat we'll face at Oklahoma is scary. We haven't had any hot days around here and out there we'll be facing unbelieveable temperatures. I wish we could practice in a sauna.

But when writers from Oklahoma called him for interviews, he said publicly, "If we get a real hot day out there, we might not be able to come out for the second half. And if we do make it for the second half, we'll probably die in the fourth quarter."

That was what Nehlen told the Oklahoma writers. "I wanted them to think that Oklahoma was going to kill us, especially in the fourth quarter. I wanted them to believe there was no way we could play in that heat," he said.

What he told his players was, "You aren't going to die in that heat at Oklahoma. If you think you are, that's a copout, a crutch, a bunch of crap. Do you know what we're going to do? We're going to go out there and play our best football, especially in the fourth quarter. They think that's when we'll die, but that's when we'll beat them."

And Nehlen and his Mountaineers visualized how they would play against the Sooners. They visualized their defense stopping the Oklahoma wishbone.

Nehlen had a big scare in pre-season drills when Hostetler injured the knee he had sprained in spring practice. Nehlen did lose offensive guard Rob Schellhaas, who tore a knee ligament and had to undergo surgery. And sophomore linebacker Derek Christian was doubtful because of a neck injury. Nehlen moaned, "We're hurting. Our defense has no intensity and the offense is bad."

Finally, it was September 11 and the Mountaineers were in Norman to face the mighty Sooners. Although the temperature was only in the low 90's, Oklahoma coach Barry Switzer was supremely confident. His Sooners were in everybody's pre-season top 10. They were favored over WVU by 24 points.

In a final tuneup the week before, the Oklahoma offense, one that led the nation in rushing the year before, had scored 34 points. A speedy sophomore fullback named Fred Sims gained 62 yards on only seven carries. A talented

225-pound freshman with 4.4 speed named Marcus Depree averaged 15 yards a carry. As usual, the Sooners had speed to burn in the backfield. And the Oklahoma offensive line averaged 270 pounds a man.

It didn't take a genius to figure that Switzer intended to run the ball against WVU.

West Virginia fans were hoping the Mountaineers "could at least make it respectable."

In the final WVU pre-season scrimmage, Hostetler showed no signs of a sore knee and completed 12 of 12 passes. He and the Mountaineers appeared to be as ready as they were ever going to be.

Three hours before the game, Nehlen met with his squad in a meeting room of the Ramada Inn, the WVU headquarters just off I-35 on the outskirts of Norman. He didn't tell the team what was really on his mind — that he thought Oklahoma was one of the fastest teams he had ever seen on film, that its quarterback ran a 9.6 in the 100, that its backs ran like they were jet-propelled, that it had its entire defense back, that it might take a miracle for the Mountaineers to win.

Instead, he told them, "Men, for heaven's sake don't get discouraged if they pop a touchdown on us early. They probably will. In fact, because of their speed, they might pop two on us. It's going to take you a little while to adjust your angles of pursuit to combat their speed.

"We've had a problem preparing to defend against their wishbone, because we didn't have any 9.6 halfbacks, or 9.6 quarterbacks on our scout team. But remember this, they didn't have anybody on their scout team who could throw the football like we can, either. We're not going out there today with our hands tied behind our backs.

"When they pop one on us early, don't look at the scoreboard. The heck with the scoreboard. You just hang in there and do the things we've worked on.

"We may not win the game in the first quarter. And we may not win it at halftime. And we may not win it in the third quarter. That's not important. What is important is that we will win the game!

"We didn't come all the way out here to lose.

"And I'll tell you this, if we can go in at the half down by only two touchdowns, we've got 'em.

"We're going to be stronger in the second half. Mark my words."

The Sooners did pop one on WVU early. In fact, the game began like it was going to be a repeat of that 52-10 beating the Mountaineers suffered in '78. In the first four minutes of play, Oklahoma fullback Weldon Ledbetter scored on a four-yard run. The Sooners led 7-0. Five minutes later, quarterback Kelly Phelps kept on the option play and scored from six yards out to make it 14-0. And it would have been 17-0 if WVU's Brad Minetree hadn't gotten a hand up to deflect an Oklahoma field goal attempt.

At the end of the first quarter, Oklahoma had rushed for 165 yards, passed for 16 more and piled up nine first downs. The Mountaineers had only one yard rushing, 14 more passing and one first down.

The Oklahoma horse and wagon had pulled that wagon around the field twice in the first 15 minutes to celebrate those touchdowns. The Sooners' faithful figured they'd see their horse quite a few more times before the afternoon was over.

Prior to the start of the second quarter, Nehlen told his players, "See, I told you they might pop a couple on us." He was keeping up a good front. He didn't want his players to panic. They had to believe.

At the same time, he was doing some mental arithmetic and thinking that if things kept going the way they were, the score might be worse than it was in 1978. He thought, "No question, it looks like it's going to be a rout."

But he was aware that his team had stopped the Sooners on their last drive at the end of the first quarter — and blocked the field goal attempt.

And sure enough, just as Nehlen predicted, the Mountaineers adjusted.

With Hostetler leading the way, West Virginia began to move the ball. In the second quarter they got on the scoreboard when Paul Woodside kicked a 26-yard field goal. Six mintues later, Hostetler found tight end Mark Raugh in the endzone for a 10-yard scoring strike.

WVU had pulled to within four points at 14-10.

With 31 seconds to go in the half and Oklahoma still leading, Hostetler threw what appeared to be his second touchdown pass — a six-yarder to wide receiver Darrell Miller. The few Mountaineer fans among the crowd of 75,008 went crazy. Sooner fans stared in disbelief.

But a holding penalty nullified the score and WVU had to settle for another Woodside field goal, this one from 38 yards out. The Mountaineers trailed by only one point, 14-13.

On the ensuing kickoff, the Mountaineers surprised the Sooners with an onside kick and Minetree recovered at the Oklahoma 33. And with 10 seconds on the clock, Hostetler called an "81 deep" pass to Miller. On the snap, Miller set sail down the sideline toward the flag. Hostetler threw a perfect high floater.

Miller caught the ball over his shoulder, did a little stutter step around the flag and went out of bounds. He said, "I looked at the referee to see if he was going to call the touchdown, because I knew I had scored. When you're playing away from home, you never know what the officials will call. Then, the ref signaled, 'Touchdown,' and, man I went into my atmospheric dance."

Incredible as it seemed, the Mountaineers went into the dressing room at halftime leading the Sooners, 20-14.

In the locker room, Nehlen told his team, "You see, men, this game is going just exactly like we said. Now, we aren't going to worry about dying in this heat in the second half. We're going to go after them."

In the second half, Oklahoma retained possession on fourth down as a result of a holding penalty against WVU and drove for a score to go up 21-20. But Hostetler came right back with touchdown passes of 30 yards to tailback Curlin Beck and nine yards to flanker Wayne Brown.

Early in the fourth quarter the Mountaineers led, 34-21.

"Then we got out of that 11-man front and went back

to our regular defense," said Nehlen. "We put safety Tim Agee back in center field where he belonged."

And in the closing minutes of the game, the Mountaineers added insult to injury by catching the Oklahoma defense, by now a shambles after the WVU aerial bombardment, on its heels. Nehlen called a draw play and Beck went through a gaping hole in the Oklahoma line 43 yards to score.

"The hole was so big I could have driven a truck through it," laughed Beck. "Nobody laid a finger on me."

The Mountaineers led, 41-27, and had completely dominated Oklahoma in the second half. They had broken the back of the famed Sooners' wishbone and forced them to go to the air.

"We knew then we had them, because they had to throw the ball and that wasn't their style," said Nehlen. "And we found out that they had trouble defending the multiple formations in our pro passing game."

After that near-disastrous first quarter when the Sooners jumped off to a 14-0 lead and held WVU to only 15 yards total offense, the Mountaineers outscored Oklahoma, 41-13, in the final three quarters. In those three quarters, WVU outgained Oklahoma, 443 yards to 239, and had 19 first downs to 11. Oklahoma's only scores in the second half came on WVU mistakes — a holding penalty and a missed block that resulted in a blocked punt.

Hostetler riddled the Oklahoma secondary with 17 completions in 37 attempts for 321 yards and four touchdowns. Beck rushed three times for 51 yards, and King Harvey carried 10 times for 47. Oklahoma quarterback Phelps tried to throw, but completed only seven of 18 for 84 yards. And talented freshman tailback Marcus Depree wasn't a factor.

The final score was: West Virginia 41, Oklahoma 27!

West Virginia had beaten the Sooners and scored the most points ever against an Oklahoma team on its home field.

Nehlen said, "We came in here with a definite game plan and didn't vary from it. We knew we could pass. Hey, we're a passing team. You know what I mean? We always will be. When I saw the way Oklahoma tried to defend against us, I knew we could go deep on them. We threw deep all day. I guarantee you, we had our passing attack in mid-season form. They didn't know how to handle it.

"When you have to come to Oklahoma with its great tradition and record, and play in this heat, and still win, well, it has to be a great, great victory.

"Normally, you can count on Oklahoma fumbling the ball a lot. Today they didn't lose one fumble. If anyone had told me before the game that Oklahoma wouldn't turn the ball over to us and we'd still beat them, I might have questioned his sanity.

"But when we got ahead in the fourth quarter, we took the Sooners out of their wishbone. You can't come from behind late in a game with the wishbone. It's too time-consuming. And you can't throw from the wishbone, either. It isn't a good offense when you have to play catch-up."

Barry Switzer said, "Maybe West Virginia is better than we thought. We knew they would complete some passes, but they beat us time and again by running the same deep routes. You could say we were victims of a bombing raid. We couldn't stop 'em.

"There are no easy teams in college football anymore. And the way West Virginia played against us, they could have beaten anyone in the country today."

The victory was called by Nehlen "West Virginia's greatest ever" and "my greatest ever." And it earned the Mountaineers the No. 15 spot in the season's first United Press International poll and a No. 17 ranking in The Associated Press poll. Also, Nehlen was named "UPI Coach of the Week." Ironically, he had been voted the same honor 10 years earlier when his Bowling Green team opened the season with a 17-14 upset of Purdue.

"We moved up that last rung of the prestige ladder," Nehlen said. Then he chuckled and added, "But I guess we won't know that we've finally arrived until people get our name right.

"I picked up a copy of the Sunday Tusla World newspaper and the headline on page one read: 'Sooners Beaten by Virginians.' You'd think we were from a foreign country.

"That's OK. We know who won."

The following Monday, West Virginia Governor Jay Rockefeller visited Mountaineer Field and offered his congratulations, saying, "Every West Virginian is proud of your accomplishment and the way you persevered against Oklahoma. The win over Oklahoma is one of the top two sporting achievements in the state in the past 50 years.

"The other one was the hiring of Don Nehlen as head coach."

Chapter Twelve

The three West Virginia State Police cars were parked on the berm in the southbound lanes of Interstate 79 at the West Virginia state line. It was well past midnight. The troopers in the cars kept looking in their rearview mirrors for any sign of the three-bus caravan they were to meet.

Finally, one trooper spotted the buses and relayed the message over the police radio to the troopers in the other cars, "Here they come."

It was the charter buses carrying Don Nehlen and his West Virginia University football team on their way home from the Greater Pittsburgh International Airport. About an hour earlier, they had arrived in Pittsburgh from Norman, Okla., on a chartered jet.

The state troopers turned on the blue flashing lights, pulled their cars onto the highway and formed a roadblock. The bus caravan came to a halt and the troopers approached the buses.

Most of the Mountaineers were asleep, or trying to make themselves as comfortable as possible in those cramped bus seats. Nehlen, in the lead bus, said to the bus driver, "What is it? Why are the police stopping us?"

The driver shrugged his shoulders. He didn't think he had been exceeding the speed limit. Oh, maybe he had been, but not by more than a few miles an hour. He didn't know why the state police had stopped them.

The driver opened the door of the bus and the first trooper said, "Where's Coach Nehlen?"

Nehlen said, "Right here. What's up?"

The trooper said, "Congratulations on that win over Oklahoma, coach. Now, how would you and your boys like a police escort from here into Morgantown? There's a big reception waiting for you at Mountaineer Field, and we're under instructions to get you there."

Nehlen laughed and said, "OK. Let's go."

The caravan, now with an unexpected escort, resumed the trip to Morgantown. When the caravan got near Mountaineer Field, there were parked cars everywhere. Thousands of fans were in the main parking lot behind the main scoreboard. Fans were running everywhere. Some ran alongside and banged on the sides of the buses.

The caravan pulled into the main parking lot and up to a hastily erected platform, complete with a microphone and loudspeaker system.

The driver of the bus carrying Nehlen opened the door again. This time there weren't two or three troopers outside. There were thousands of fans. They chanted, "We want Coach Nehlen! We want Coach Nehlen!"

Nehlen said, "This is great." But he said to himself,

"I'm almost afraid to go out there. It's 1 a.m. Some of those guys out there might be juiced up. I'm liable to get hurt."

But he got out of the bus, or tried to get out of the bus. When he appeared on the steps, the fans picked him up and carried him on their shoulders to the platform for a 'victory speech.'

"That was quite a night," Nehlen said. "I've been greeted by fans before after a big win, but nothing like this. The whole scene was just unbelieveable. Dynamite! The fans were cheering, yelling and whooping it up. And our players were up in the clouds for the second time in a little over eight hours."

The first time had been right after their big 41-27 upset of Oklahoma.

On Monday afternoon, though, Nehlen was through celebrating. He was all business. After the governor's appearance following practice, Nehlen told his players, "Men, it's time we quit patting ourselves on the backs. All we did was go out to Oklahoma and win a football game. So what? We knew before we went out to Oklahome that we were a good football team. Hey, good teams expect to win.

"So you beat Oklahoma. What's to get excited about? You'd better be getting excited about Maryland this week and forget about Oklahoma."

Nehlen added, "I was as happy as the kids were. Jiminy Christmas, I had been voted 'Coach of the something-or-other.' Everybody was patting us on the backs. My coaching buddies were calling me on the phone and saying, 'Don, how could you guys beat Oklahoma at Norman? How in Sam Hill did you guys score 41 points on them out there? What in the heck did you do?'

"I think our win over the Sooners blew their minds."

Certainly, Nehlen would have loved to let his players bask in the glow of that tremendous victory a little longer. He probably wouldn't have minded enjoying it a while longer himself. He knew what his players had accomplished on the hot artificial turf at Oklahoma. He knew what a boost that win was for his program. And he knew that he and his coaching staff had done a masterful job of preparing the team to play the Sooners.

But Nehlen was even more aware of the chore facing him, his staff and his players this week. "I had to get them back to earth and get them ready for Maryland," he said. "Maryland was a must if we were to achieve any success at all."

He had forced himself down out of the clouds. His

desk was piled high with calls from fans wanting to offer congratulations. "If I had wanted to," Nehlen said, I could have spent a couple of days doing nothing but talking on the phone about Oklahoma. I just had to ignore most of the calls, because if I hadn't, I wouldn't have found time to coach. I know some coaches who don't do much coaching, but I'm not one of them.

"I told them, 'We're a good team, but are we mature? This is the week we find that out. If we can't get past Maryland, then what the heck good was that victory over Oklahoma? That game is past and in the win column. This week is the real test. Can we handle this success? Can we keep from falling on our faces?"

It was going to be a difficult task to get the Mountaineers ready for Maryland in the home opener that Saturday at Mountaineer Field. Maryland promised to be as big and tough as usual. With the strength program former Terrapins' Coach Jerry Clairborne had instituted three years ago, Maryland prided itself on being strong and physical.

The Terps had a new coach in Bobby Ross, a former assistant coach of the Kansas City Chiefs of the National Football League. It was obvious that Ross had continued the strength program, because the same day that West Virginia upended Oklahoma, Maryland opened at Penn State and lost in a close battle, 39-31, after leading 21-20 late in the third quarter.

West Virginia had edged Maryland the year before at College Park, 17-13, when they scored the winning touchdown after the Terps fumbled a punt in the final minutes.

"Maryland had quarterback Boomer Esiason back," said Nehlen. "In 1981 he completed a school record 122 passes. He completed 15 of them against us. We knew if we weren't ready to play, we'd be in for a long afternoon."

It was a long afternoon. On a cloudy day in front of a standing-room-only crowd of 56,042, the Mountaineers and Maryland squared off in what proved to be another thriller. West Virginia trailed at the half, 9-6. Its points came on two Paul Woodside field goals. A third Woodside field goal in the third quarter tied it at 9-9, before Maryland took a 12-9 lead with a field goal of its own.

Then at the start of the fourth quarter Jeff Hostetler threw a 35-yard touchdown pass to Rich Hollins. WVU led, 16-12. And four minutes later, Woodside booted a fourth field goal for a 19-12 lead.

With 7:20 to go in the game, Maryland marched 75 yards to score. And with 1:39 to play, the Terps trailed by only a point, 19-18. They lined up to go for two points to win the game.

And as Nehlen had done so many times in his first two seasons at WVU, he gambled. He said, "We guessed Esiasan was going to throw for the two points. So, we blitzed both our outside linebackers. We figured both of Maryland's tight ends would go out for the pass. Also, we figured even if both their ends didn't go out, at least one of them would. That meant one of our linebackers wasn't going to get blocked.

"Now, if Maryland kept both its ends in to block, then we guessed wrong. But we were certain they would go

with their Esiason throwing for the two points. He was their big gun.

"We guessed right. Esiason tried to throw off some kind of play-action pass. One tight end went one way, and the other cut across the middle. When that end went across the middle, it freed up Darryl Talley (WVU's All-American outside linebacker) to come blowing in.

"Esiason turned to throw the ball and there was Talley right in his face. Boom! Esiason had to release the ball sooner than he wanted to and threw it high and out of the end zone. Esiason's receiver had no chance to catch the ball."

And West Virginia had victory No. 2, a 19-18 squeaker over Maryland. And the Mountaineers, who broke into the top 20 polls the week before after that Oklahoma win, moved up one notch in one wire service poll (from 15th to 14th by United Press International) and two notches in the other poll (from 17th to 15th by the Associated Press).

Afterward, Nehlen said, "A lot of folks will never know what a big win this one was. It takes a pretty confident and mature football team to do what this one has done in the last two weeks — go out to Oklahoma and win, and then come back and beat this Maryland team. The team is getting experience against the top programs in the country. Experience breeds confidence, and confidence breeds success.

"Now, our offensive line isn't what I want it to be. It probably won't ever be as good as I want it. I'm never satisfied. But I'll tell you this, I'm proud of my kids. They are giving 100 percent, and are going to get better."

The Richmond Spiders were next.

Nehlen had a seemingly impossible job to tell his players that Richmond was a dangerous team and capable of upsetting them. The Mountaineers could read. They were aware that Richmond was winless.

"They weren't aware, though, that in recent years West Virginia had 'clobbered' Richmond by such huge scores as 9-6, 14-12, 20-18 and 31-28," said Nehlen. "I had to somehow convince the team not to take Richmond lightly."

Richmond Coach Dal Shealy certainly wasn't taking West Virginia lightly. He wished he didn't have to take them at all. He said, "Are we underdogs? That's the dumbest question I ever heard. The polls have West Virginia ranked 14th. They ought to be about No. 5. I saw in the polls that Florida was ranked that high. Didn't West Virginia beat Florida in the Peach Bowl last year? Darn right they did. Well, they ought to be right up there with Florida.

"West Virginia is an explosive team. You can hold them, and hold them — and then, 'bang,' they'll hit a bomb on you. They'll bomb you to death."

Shealy was almost wrong. The Mountaineers didn't bomb the Spiders to death. They hit on only one — a 44-yarder from Hostetler to Hollins. But West Virginia did rush for 223 yards and Hostetler scored three times on one-yard quarterback sneaks. Woodside rounded out the scoring with three field goals in the 43-10 romp.

Nehlen commented, "We beat Richmond like we were

supposed to. But if I had my way, we wouldn't play a team like that. We scored on our first five possessions and led 33-3 at the half. And we scored on our first possession in the third quarter. After that, I took my starters out of the game — all of them."

The WVU coach angrily explained, "We had two guys (center Bill Legg and tackle Ernie Anderson) suffer knee injuries. Those Richmond guys were driving at our kids' legs. That's not the way to block. Our kids were more worried about getting their knees hurt than they were about playing football. Richmond was chop blocking our kids. If I had my way, we wouldn't play teams that do that. I'm just glad it's over and we didn't get anybody else hurt."

On Monday after the Richmond win, ABC-TV announced it would regionally televise the unbeaten Mountaineers' next game against arch-rival Pitt at Pitt. It was to be West Virginia's second television apprence in the last five regular season games, and counting the nationally televised Peach Bowl, it was the third network appearance in the last six games.

"Pitt is probably the most talented football team in the country," said Nehlen. "And I'm not the only one who thinks so." Pitt, unbeaten in three games, was ranked No. 1 in one poll and No. 2 in the other. WVU was 14th in both.

Nehlen tried his best to convince his players that "it will be fun" playing at Pitt. One thing was certain, the WVU coach would find out how good his players were. His philosophy had always been to make certain his teams beat the teams they were supposed to beat, and to take good shots at the better teams.

"When we play Pitt," he said, "we'll be taking a shot at one of the big boys. The game will be televised. There will be no problem motivating my players. Our kids like the exposure. I like it. I might even have to go out and buy some hair spray."

West Virginia's big problem was going to be protecting quarterback Jeff Hostetler from the terrific Pitt pass rush. In three games, the Panthers had sacked opposing quarterbacks 17 times. The young Mountaineers' offensive line was going to be tested. So was their defense in trying to stop Pitt's talented quarterback, Dan Marino.

It was a sunny day in Pitt Stadium, and an overflow crowd of 57,250 turned out to watch the 75th game in the old rivalry.

West Virginia got on the scoreboard first when Woodside booted a 34-yard field goal midway in the first quarter. That was the only scoring in the first half and WVU went off at intermission leading, 3-0. Jim Merritts, WVU's defensive tackle, thwarted Pitt's only scoring threat in the first 30 minutes when he broke through to block a field goal attempt.

On the third play of the third quarter, Darryl Talley intercepted a Marino pass at the Pitt 33 and returned it to the 13. Four plays later, Woodside booted a 29-yard field goal to make it, 6-0. It was Woodside's 15th field goal in a row, two shy of the NCAA record for consecutive field goals.

And on the third play of the final quarter, Pitt was forced to punt from its own 22. Tally roared in to block the punt and recovered it in the end zone for a West Virginia touchdown. Woodside kicked the extra point and WVU led, 13-0.

There was 14:08 to play. And to this point, Pitt's deepest penetration, aside from the blocked field goal from the 16-yard line in the first quarter, had been to the WVU 31. A field goal try from there was wide.

Pitt took the ensuing kickoff and drove 83 yards in 10 plays to make it, 13-7.

Then came the turning point in the game. With 5:30 remaining in the game, the Mountaineers were deep in their own territory. First down from the eight-yard line. Hostetler ran for 11 yards and a first down, then ran 24 yards up the middle for another first down. West Virginia had moved the ball out to its 45. First down. If the Mountaineers could keep the drive alive, the clock would be in their favor.

On the previous play, West Virginia center Dave Johnson had been hurt and had to leave the game. Bill Legg, who had been injured in the previous week's win, had to take over.

The Mountaineers lined up. Hostetler came up to the line of scrimmage, called the signals. Legg snapped the ball — and Hostetler fumbled it! Pitt recovered. The Panthers had possession at the WVU 48 with plenty of time to score, and they did to go ahead, 14-13. And with 41 seconds left in the game, the Panthers' furious pass rush sacked Hostetler in the end zone for a safety. Now Pitt led, 16-13.

West Virginia was forced to kick off, and Nehlen gambled on an onside kick. Woodside executed it perfectly and the Mountaineers recovered at their 31. Hostetler moved WVU to the Pitt 36 in three plays. Seven seconds remained when Woodside tried a 52-yard field goal to tie the score.

It was on line, but went under the crossbar as the final second ticked off the clock. West Virginia had suffered its first defeat of the season, 16-13.

Pitt Coach Foge Fazio knew his panthers were lucky to get out of that game alive. He said, "I take my hat off to Don Nehlen and his West Virginia team. That is one hellava football team."

After the game, Hostetler, who had taken 17 hits from the brutal Panthers' pass rush, had to be helped to the team bus. WVU trainer Greg Ott listed the quarterback's ailment as "complete exhaustion and a bruised body."

"Jeff Hostetler gave one of the guttiest performance I've ever seen," said Nehlen in the post-game interview. "Obviously, having to change centers late in the fourth quarter hurt us. I'm just thankful Jeff wore a flak jacket. If he hadn't, he might have been killed. Can you believe it? Pitt hit him 17 times after he threw the ball and was called for roughing the passer only twice.

"But the thing that really hurt us was when Talley blocked that punt for the touchdown at the start of the fourth quarter. That put us up, 12-0. Now, 12-0 wasn't what we wanted. We wanted to make it 14-0. The situation dictated that we go for a two-point conversion. I turned around to find my extra point team and can't find any of them. They are all down in the end zone pounding on Talley's back and jumping up and down. Our sideline was pure bedlam.

"Hell, everybody knows you are supposed to go for two points, and we can't get it done. We had to settle for one point. That hurt. We started celebrating too soon and it cost us.

"After that, our guys looked at the scoreboard, which I tell them never to do. They said to themselves, 'We've got this game won. All we have to do is hang on.' And they went tentative. Suddenly, instead of playing to win, they started playing to lose. And we blew it.

"Yes, I said blew it. Pitt didn't beat us. We beat ourselves. No question about it, we had played inspired football until we got that 13-0 lead. After that we fell apart."

And Nehlen lectured his players the following day at the Sunday team meeting about what had happened in the fourth quarter. He told them, "There we were. We had it! And you guys went crazy. How many times have I told you to never look at the score board? How many times have I told you to play every play like it's the last one? How many times have I told you the game isn't over until it's over?

"You and I know we should have won that game. We momentarily lost our composure and it cost us one heckuva big victory."

To his coaches, Nehlen said, "From now on we're going to use what hapened to us at Pitt as a teaching tool. We knew this would happen some time, because this team is still suffering growing pains. Now we have to make sure that in the long run what happened to us at Pitt helps us."

There was no time for the Mountaineers to lick their wounds. Boston College, 3-0-1 and ranked 19th in the polls, was next. WVU fell to 16th and 17th in the polls. Fortunately, the game was at Mountaineer Field. It was homecoming and a capacity crowd of 55,554 was on hand.

Boston College scout Buck O'Connor, who scouted the Mountaineers at Pitt, said, "I scouted West Virginia the year before when it beat Colorado State, 49-3. I underestimated the Mountaineers and they beat us, 38-10. That was my fault. I can tell you this, we aren't underestimating them this year. We're a pretty good team and our guys will be ready to play. Quarterback Doug Flutie gives our team a whole new dimension. He does for us what Hostetler does for West Virginia."

What was to have been a battle of quarterbacks turned into a defensive struggle. Hostetler completed only 11 of 29 passes for 98 yards and Flutie hit only nine of 33 for 122 yards. The only scoring in the first half came on field goals — two by Woodside and one by Boston College. WVU led, 6-3.

In the second half, Boston College tied it on a 25-yard field goal. West Virginia's Willie Drewey returned the ensuing kickoff 39 yards to the WVU 41. In nine plays the Mountaineers moved to the Boston College 37. There the

drive stalled and Steve Superick punted. Three plays later, WVU's Dave Oblak intercepted a Flutie pass at the Boston College 33 and returned it to the 22.

Hostetler passed 19 yards to freshman tailback Tommy Gray. And then on the next play, Gray carried off left tackle for the touchdown. Woodside booted the point and WVU led, 13-6.

In the fourth quarter, Boston College tied the score with a touch down on an eight-yard pass off of a fake field goal play.

With one minute to play, WVU was faced with a fourth down and 10 from its own 37. If the Mountaineers punted, it was very likely they wouldn't get the ball back and the game would end in a 13-13 tie.

Nehlen said, "Punt the ball."

A year earlier, he had ordered his Mountaineers to punt the ball in the closing minutes of the game at Maryland. They had questioned the call and "wanted to go for it." Nehlen prevailed and WVU punted. Maryland fumbled the punt, the Mountaineers recovered the ball and went on to win the game, 17-13.

"This time when I ordered my team to punt," Nehlen said, "there were no stares from the players like they thought I was loony. They believed in what we were trying to do. The difference in the Maryland game a year ago and this one was that now my team wanted to punt the ball.

"I remember when I sent the punting unit on the field against Boston College, fullback Tommy Bowman came over to me and said, 'We'll get the ball back, coach. We'll get it back on this play.' "

Superick got off a high, spiraling 51-yard punt. and the Mountaineers' punt team raced down field to converge on the Boston College punt returner — and he fumbled the punt, and Bowman recovered at the Boston College 13-yard line. And with 25 seconds remaining in the game, Hostetler scored on a quarterback keeper.

West Virginia had bounced back from the Pitt defeat and won, 20-13. The Mountaineers' record was 4-1.

Nehlen said, "Sure there was some luck involved in the game. If their guy hadn't fumbled, we wouldn't have had the chance to recover the ball. But the important point is, our kids believed something would happen, and it did.

"That was the difference. Now the kids believed. A year ago when I made that decision to punt against Maryland, nobody on my team thought I was very smart. One year later, the team never questioned my decision. They knew I was going to have them punt. They expected it. And instead of pleading to 'go for it' on fourth down, they said, 'We'll get it back.' That's what maturing, believing in defense and believing in special teams can do for you.

"Finally, my thinking had been ingrained in my players. We were all on the same page now."

On Oct. 16 the Mountaineers were scheduled to play Virginia Tech at Blacksburg, Va. But four days before the game Nehlen had to dispell a rumor that he was a candidate to replace Earl Bruce at Ohio State. Bruce's Buckeyes had just suffered their third consecutive home defeat, 6-0, to Wisconsin. And the rumor was that Bruce was going to get axed.

Nehlen said, "Why does something like this have to come up at this time? First of all, Earl Bruce is a great coach and a very personal friend of mine. And second, if I weren't happy at West Virginia, I wouldn't be here. Why does everybody use my name every time there's a rumor that a head coaching job might be open?"

And the rumor was just that — a rumor.

As a result of the win over Boston College, Nehlen's Mountaineers climbed to No. 12 in the UPI poll and No. 13 in the AP poll. Nehlen, a member of the UPI coaches' poll committee, was asked where he voted his Mountaineers in the poll. He said, "Just say I voted for us. I ain't telling you where. I don't get excited about polls, but I am happy for the players. They have worked hard and are deserving."

Although Nehlen tried to play down the importance of the polls, he knew what was at stake for his team. A win over Virginia Tech would give the Mountaineers a 5-1 record, enable them to keep their national ranking and put them in position for an outstanding season. "Tech is a big, big game for us," Nehlen said. "But every game we play is the biggest game of the season. I just wonder how many times I can tell my players that?

"The Oklahoma game was big. The Maryland game was big. The Pitt game was big. The Boston College game was big. And now Tech is 'THE GAME.' "

West Virginia hadn't won at Blacksburg since 1974. "I don't care about that bull," said Nehlen, refusing to answer any questions about a possible jinx. "Our players know what's at stake. They'll handle it."

The Mountaineers handled it, and beat Tech, 16-6, despite a gusting 25-mile-an-hour wind. The wind moved WVU near the top 10 in the polls (11th in UPI and 13th in AP). But the victory was costly. Quarterback Jeff Hostetler suffered a sprained big toe. That was on top of the bumps and bruises he had received against Pitt, the ankle he sprained in practice, and the mononucleosis he was recovering from. The mono had only recently been diagnosed.

"Jeff isn't getting any better," said Nehlen. "In fact, he's very sick. But we play Penn State next and I'll probably have to shoot him to keep him out of the lineup."

For Hostetler, who transferred to WVU from Penn State two years earlier, this would be his first appearance against his former teammates.

The largest crowd in WVU history (60,958) turned out at Mountaineer Field that week to see the Mountaineers take on the ninth-ranked Nittany Lions. It would be Hostetler vs. Penn State quarterback Todd Blackledge. This would be the year the Mountaineers would snap that long string of Penn State victories over them.

Why not? The Mountaineers had won at Oklahoma, hadn't they? If they could win there, they should be able to beat Penn State at home.

Nehlen said, "I don't believe in jinxes. We haven't beaten Penn State for years because our program hasn't been as good as theirs. This time? I don't know. All I know is they are a son-of-a-gun of a team. Now, don't get me

wrong. We're pretty good, too. But right now, we're not in the best of shape."

The Mountaineers weren't. They moved the ball up and down the field against Penn State, but every time they got to the Penn State 20, they committed a turnover. Hostetler was intercepted three times and WVU lost one fumble.

Penn State capitalized on the errors and walked away with a 24-0 victory, its 24th consecutive win over the Mountaineers.

Afterward, Nehlen said, "We moved the ball pretty well. But when we made a mistake, it was a colossal one. It was a tough defeat. We had 21 first downs to Penn State's 18, and 382 yards total offense to Penn State's 343. Yet, we don't score a point and they get 24. Crazy game, huh?

"But this game proved to our kids what we've been trying to tell them about turnovers, that they'll kill you. Turnovers are the name of the game. You simply cannot turn the ball over against a good football team and expect to win the game. I think our kids got a lesson in the importance of turnovers today.

"In all games, win, lose, or draw, you learn a lot."

The loss dropped the Mountainers to 17th and 18th in the polls.

After the Penn State game, the injuries caught up with Hostetler, and he missed the next two games. Sophomore quarterback Kevin White replaced Hostetler and was equal to the task. He quarterbacked the Mountaineers over East Carolina, 30-3, and Temple, 20-17.

Nehlen debated starting Hostetler against Temple, but changed his mind. "Hostetler proably could have played," Nehlen said. "But we wanted to get him 100 percent well. I made a mistake and played him against Penn State. He shouldn't have played that game. I wasn't about to make the same mistake twice."

There were six bowl scouts on hand the day in Philadelphia's Veterans Stadium when the Mountaineers squeaked past Temple. They were from the Gator, Liberty, Peach, Fiesta, Tangerine and Hall of Fame bowls. WVU Athletic Director Fred Schaus said after the game, "How important was this game? Well, it was probably a $400,000 game."

What Schaus meant was that WVU, now with a 7-2 record, was being considered for a second straight bowl game. "All those scouts certainly didn't come to Philadelphia to see us lose," he said.

Nehlen had his usual response to the early bowl talk. He had been hearing bowl rumors for more than a week, even that a matchup between his Mountaineers and North Carolina was proposed for the Liberty Bowl in Memphis.

He said, "Yeah, I know there were bowl scouts up in the press box watching us when we played Temple. I'm not stupid. My kids aren't either. But I don't know what the bowl scouts look for when they watch a team play. Honestly, I don't think those scouts know enough to know what I look for. I've found that if you keep winning, the bowls take care of themselves. All we have to do is keep winning. I refuse to talk about bowls."

Nehlen wasn't exactly truthful about refusing to talk

about bowls, because at his Sunday squad meeting prior to the next-to-last game of the season — a game against Rutgers moved to Thursday night in the Meadowlands to accomodate television (the game was to be televised on national cable by WTBS) — he mentioned what was at stake. But he didn't have to tell the Mountaineers. They already knew.

Seven bowls indicated they were interested in WVU. They were the Gator, Liberty, Fiesta, Peach, Tangerine, Sun and Hall of Fame bowls. If we don't beat Rutgers," Nehlen said, "the only bowl we'll be going to is the toilet bowl."

A healthy Hostetler returned to action against Rutgers, and he threw touchdownn passes for 43 and 54 yards to Rich Hollins. Willie Drewrey returned a punt 75 yards for a touchdown. Paul Woodside booted three field goals. And the Mountaineers romped over the Scarlet Knights, 44-17, in their biggest offensive display of the season. West Virginia's record was 8-2 and it moved up three places in the polls — from 17th to 14th in UPI and from 19th to 16th in AP.

Nehlen said, "We finally exploded and put some points on the board. As for the bowls, all I can say is right now there aren't too many teams out there with eight victories. One of our goals this year was to go to a bowl again. That would make two in a row, something no West Virginia team has ever done."

The following Monday the 'unofficial' word was out. All signs pointed toward the Mountaineers going to the Dec. 30 Gator Bowl in Jacksonville, Fla., against Coach Bobby Bowden's Florida Gators.

After the word was out that WVU was heading to a second consecutive bowl, a rumor began circulating that Nehlen was again being considered as a replacement for a vacant coaching position at another school. This time it was Michigan State, which had fired Coach Frank 'Muddy' Waters a few days earlier. Fred Schaus confirmed Michigan State had contacted him and "asked for permission to talk to Nehlen."

Nehlen called the report "just a rumor." He said, "I wish that stuff wouldn't get started again. I don't know any more than anyone else does. All I know is I picked up the newspaper and saw my name and Michigan State's in the same story. I haven't talked to Michigan State and don't plan to. I am coach of the Mountaineers. And right now, I'm busy worrying about our last game coming up this week."

That game was a home game against the Syracuse Orangemen, a team a Nehlen-coached West Virginia team had never beaten. And Nehlen impressed on his team the importance of the game. "Last year we ended the regular season by losing at Syracuse," he said. "That left a sour taste in all our mouths. Let's end this season with a sweet taste. Let's forget about all this bowl talk and go out and play our best.

"Last year Syracuse embarassed us. I was embarrassed as a coach. We owe these guys one. We've got eight jewels in our crown. If we beat these guys today, we'll have

number nine. Nine wins. The third best team in the history of the university. The third best. You got it. All right, let's go have some fun."

There was no way the Mountaineers could forget about the bowl talk. The word was now official. They were headed to the Gator Bowl, and the bowl bid didn't hinge on them beating Syracuse. And the word was that West Virginia would play the loser of the Florida State-LSU game.

And the Mountaineers did have fun. This time Syracuse didn't spoil West Virginia's bowl bid celebration, because the Mountaineers went on the Mountaineer Field AstroTurf and blanked the Orangemen, 26-0. Hostetler hit Drewrey with a 68-yard touchdown pass and Woodside kicked four field goals to give him an NCAA record 28 field goals in 31 attempts for the season.

"Woody is like money in the bank," said Nehlen. "From inside 40 yards he was 23-for-23. You can't get any better than that. And remember, one of his misses was that 52-yard attempt in the last-second of the Pitt game. The guy is uncanny."

West Virginia ended the regular season 9-2. It was only the third time in school history that a Mountaineer football team won nine games in the regular season. It was the first time a team had won nine games in consecutive seasons. It was the first time a team had gone to two straight bowls.

The following week the Mountaineers cracked the top 10 in the wire service polls. They were moved up to No. 8 in the UPI poll and No. 10 in the AP poll. It was the first time in history that a WVU team had been ranked in the polls for an entire season. And for the first time, home attendance at WVU football games exceeded the seating capacity of the field. The Mountaineers averaged 53,348 in 50,500-seat Mountaineer Field.

Nehlen said, "I've always said that the only poll that counts is the final one that comes out after the bowl games. I still feel that way. But I also know that television folks look at the polls, and where you are in the polls determines whether you get on television. Bowl people look at the polls, too. If you are high in the polls, you stand a better chance of going to a bowl.

"If you are high in the polls, it means you are having a great season. So, I guess it goes hand in hand. Being in the top 10 is a great boost to our program.

"You know, when I took this job I figured it would take about five years to get the job done. This is our third season, so I guess you could say we are little ahead of schedule. Maybe we've had a little luck. I don't know. But I do know that we get more out of our kids, sometimes more than they have to give.

"How have we won? I honestly don't know. We've worked hard. But coaches all over the country work hard. We've recruited pretty well. But I know a lot of coaches who recruit well. Our facilities are great. There are plenty of other universities with great facilities.

"Heck, I don't know. Maybe we have been lucky."

Chapter Thirteen

Don Nehlen sat in a lounge chair on the balcony of his top floor suite in the Treasure Island Inn in Daytona Beach, Fla. His perch gave him a perfect view of the white sands of the seemingly endless beach and the awesome expanse of the Atlantic Ocean.

It was two days before Christmas 1982.

But he wasn't in Daytona Beach for a holiday of sun and sand. This trip wasn't a vacation. He was there to prepare his Mountaineers to go against Florida State the next week in the 38th annual Gator Bowl in Jacksonville, Fla.

Nehlen sat there with his feet propped up and reflected on the sudden success of his football program — two consecutive nine-victory seasons, a second straight appearance in a bowl, a finish in the nation's top 20 the year before and a lofty position in the top 10 this year.

He said, "I've never professed to know an awful lot about the game of football, because I'm not that smart. But I think I know something about discipline and winning. I've been associated with some fine head coaches and I've learned that there are characteristics of teams and characteristics of people, winning characteristics and losing characteristics.

"I learned from Bo Schembechler during my three years as an assistant coach on his Michigan staff that with discipline, you have a chance to win. Without discipline, you have no chance. You must have discipline above all else. Everyone needs discipline. And I honestly believe that kids today want discipline.

"If there's one thing that irks me in my visits to high schools on recruiting trips, it's that teachers in classrooms have no discipline. They don't create an atmosphere for learning. That's wrong.

"If I were a principal of a high school and I had a teacher who had no discipline, I'd fire him on the spot, because he wouldn't be doing his job. Kids love discipline. They want somebody to take charge.

"Criminy, without discipline you could never accomplish a thing. As I look back on my early career as a college head coach at Bowling Green, I realize I wasn't a very good coach. Maybe I was too gung-ho. And I probably had a few discipline problems. I don't know. But I do know that my teams now are disciplined. That will never be a problem.

"At West Virginia I may not be able to coach, but my players will damn sure know who the coach is."

A little more than 24 hours later, Nehlen was faced with putting his discipline credo into action. Two of his football players, junior tight end Fred Charles and freshman inside linebacker Van Richardson, weren't in their rooms when his assistant coaches made the 1 a.m. bed check. They were out past curfew, and had violated one of Nehlen's cardinal rules.

Nehlen met with the two players and said, "You know the rules, and broke them. Tomorrow morning at 8 a.m. you guys are going to be on an airplane heading home."

The players didn't plead. They knew it wouldn't do any good. They had broken the rules, and had been caught. But they did shed a few tears, because now they wouldn't be making the trip to Jacksonville in a few days. And they wouldn't be suiting up for the Gator Bowl with the rest of their teammates the night of Dec. 30.

Nehlen said, "What the kids did wasn't any big deal. They were out fooling around. I think they were dropping balloons filled with water off the balcony of the hotel. But that wasn't the point. The point was they broke curfew, and that was it. No ifs, ands or buts, I had to send them home. I had no choice."

Fortunately for Nehlen, one of the players was just a backup and the other probably wouldn't have seen any action.

"Now, what would I have done if one of the curfew violators had been starting quarterback Jeff Hostetler?" Nehlen said. "Well, Hostetler would have been on the plane at 8 a.m. the next morning heading home. Then I would have gone to my room, locked the door, pulled the curtains and sat down and cried a little myself."

There was one thing certain: Nehlen's quick action in sending the two players home got the attention of the rest of his squad real fast. "We didn't have any problems after that," said the head coach.

"But I wish all I had to do was coach the team. That would be simple. But that's only part of the job. I have to be a mother, father, policeman, counselor and psychologist, too. It's really easy once it gets down to X's and O's. It's the rest that's tough."

Part of Nehlen's reasoning for taking the Mountaineers to Daytona Beach prior to Christmas came as a result of what happened to Michigan in the 1979 Gator Bowl. Although Nehlen had already accepted the WVU head coaching job, he fulfilled his commitment to the Wolverines by staying with them through the bowl. Michigan lost to North Carolina, 17-15. And part of his reasoning came about because he knew the Mountaineers weren't going to surprise the Florida State the way they had Florida in the Peach Bowl the season before.

"I knew that North Carolina had gone down early and trained in Daytona Beach," he said. "Dick Crum (North Carolina head coach) really did a great job of preparing his team. I decided after Michigan was beaten by North Carolina, that if I ever took a team to the Gator Bowl, I wouldn't make the same mistake Michigan did. I'd get them out of Jacksonville for a few days, away from all the bowl hoopla."

So, when the Mountaineers got the Gator Bowl bid, Nehlen telephoned Crum and asked him what he did. Crum explained that he had gone to Daytona Beach and worked out on one of the local high school fields. Nehlen even went so far as to stay at the same hotel North Carolina did, and practice on the same field.

"You have to understand," he said, "we had to be in Jacksonville a week before the game. They had some sort of bowl banquet that we had to attend. We had to go down early. Crum told me the year he played Michigan in the Gator Bowl that he took his players to Daytona Beach where they relaxed, romped on the beach and got in a couple of light practices. He said, 'Then, when we went to Jacksonville, we were ready to get down to serious business. It worked out pretty good for us."

"So, I thought we would do the same thing."

The plan seemed to work to perfection, because the West Virginia practices in Daytona Beach were "sensational." The Mountaineers got down to business and were really smacking each other around. There were even a few fights during drills. One fight between tackles Brian Jozwiak and Jeff Lucas was so spirited that Nehlen and his coaches had difficulty pulling the players apart.

Football coaches love it when a few of their players mix it up. Nehlen explained, "A small scuffle always helps to jack up the rest of your squad. It tends to generate enthusiasm. And believe me, we had enthusiasm. In fact, I couldn't believe the way we practiced down there. I said to myself, 'You gotta be kidding me! Boy, these guys are really ready to get after Florida State."

The practices in Daytona Beach were a marked improvement from the Mountaineers' first bowl workout back in Morgantown in the school's new shell building a week earlier. "We ran our first play and one of our linemen fell down," laughed Nehlen. "I thought, 'Well, nothing has changed."

On Christmas Eve, Nehlen had a Christmas party for the team. The players received blue and gold traveling bags, sweaters, shirts, caps and watches, all compliments of the Gator Bowl. Later, they would receive official Gator Bowl rings. The next day the team bused to nearby Orlando and saw the annual Christmas Day parade at Disney World.

The next day Nehlen and the Mountaineers headed for Jacksonville. Except for the one little discipline problem, everything had gone smoothly in Daytona Beach. The players had relaxed, romped on the beach, had a party, gone to Disney World and had rough-and-tumble practices.

"I'll never forget," said Nehlen, "one day at Daytona, I looked out the window of my hotel room and saw my quarterback (Hostetler) racing up and down the beach on a motorcycle. Then I saw about a dozen of my players making a human pyramid out there on the beach. Kids will be kids, you know.

Anyhow, I just closed the curtains and said a little prayer, 'Please, Lord, don't let any of them kill themselves.' "

The first two days in Jacksonville the Mountaineers' practices were still "sensational."

Since the game was going to be a night game, Nehlen wanted at least one workout under the Gator Bowl lights. The OK for that workout didn't come until Tuesday afternoon. Nehlen was told, "You can work out under the lights tonight."

The WVU head coach wasn't too keen about that since his players had already had one practice that day. But he did feel it was important to let his players see how the lights were and get the feel of the natural turf.

Nehlen said, "Gee whiz, I didn't know what to do. I finally decided that we ought to go out in shorts and run around on the field a little. It was no big deal. And our kids went out under those lights and were super.

"My quarterback was throwing the ball a mile. My field goal kicker was kicking the ball a mile. My punter was punting the ball a mile. And it was the most beautiful, gorgeous night that you could ever imagine. No wind. No clouds. The stars were out.

"We ran a few plays and our kids were so sharp they could have cut the grass. I blew my whistle to tell the team it was time to go in. After all, our basketball team was playing against North Carolina State that night in the Meadowlands in New Jersey, and the game was being shown on closed-circuit television in a pavilion on the beach. I thought our guys would like to see that game.

"After the practice, I told my coaches, 'I've never seen the team sharper. We're ready to play the game tonight. Now what in the heck are we going to do with them for the next 48 hours?' "

Nehlen knew this was Tuesday night, and that the game wasn't to be played until Thursday night. He had a funny feeling, because he knew that when a team peaks and is ready to play, you had better play.

Nehlen knew, too, that there would be more than 20,000 Mountaineer fans in the 80,913 Gator Bowl seats the night of the game. He was aware that Mountaineer fans had bought up West Virginia's 20,000 ticket allotment in five hours, and that WVU President E. Gordon Gee had tried in vain to get 5,000 to 10,000 more tickets. West Virginia travel agencies were booked solid. The fans were wild about Nehlen and his 'Eers.'

The Gator Bowl people were amazed. West Virginia had sold its allotment of tickets faster than any other team they had ever invited to compete in the bowl.

Nehlen attempted to dispel his fears about his team's peaking too soon. After all, he had a veteran in quarterback Hostetler. He had the best field goal kicker in the nation in Woodside. He had a first-team All-American on defense in outside linebacker Darryl Talley. And he didn't think the Mountaineers would beat themselves. The team was No. 1 in the country in turnover margin.

The next time the Mountaineers went out on the Gator Bowl turf it was game night — Dec. 30. And it wasn't a gorgeous night. In fact, Nehlen said, "I couldn't have ordered worse weather, because I probably would have screwed up the order. It was raining cats and dogs. And it was foggy and cold.

"You know, it's a funny thing, but I believe that when Florida kids have to play a game like that in Florida, they just say, 'Well, here's that crazy Florida weather again. Let's go play.'

"But when northern kids go to Florida to play in a bowl, they expect to get a suntan and play in warm weather. Their reaction to a night like we had in the Gator Bowl is, 'It's raining! It can't be raining. This is Florida. It's supposed to be nice and warm.'

"That's not a copout. It's a fact of life. And it was just amazing, the spark the team had two nights before the game was gone. The night we played Florida State we were a very average football team."

The average football team won the toss, took the opening kickoff and marched 77 yards in nine plays. With a fourth down and eight yards to go from the Florida State 19, Woodside went back to attempt a 35-yard field goal. And it was blocked!

It was the first time all year that Woodside had had a field goal attempt blocked.

On WVU's next possession, the Mountaineers were forced to punt from their own 28. Steve Superick went back to punt. And it was blocked!

It was the first time all season that Superick had had a punt blocked.

Nehlen thought, "Uh oh, I don't like the looks of this. Jiminy Christmas, what's going on out there?"

What was going on was that Bowden's Seminoles were beating the Mountaineers to the punch. And by halftime Florida State led, 17-6. Two minutes into the third quarter, Willie Drewrey returned a Seminole punt 82 yards before being hauled down from behind at the Florida State seven-yard line.

It was the first time return specialist Drewrey had ever been caught from behind. And a minute later when Woodside missed a 32-yard field goal attempt, his first miss that year from inside 40 yards, Nehlen uttered another "Uh Oh!"

In the next nine minutes, Florida State scored two more touchdowns against the sluggish WVU defense and led, 31-6. The Mountaineers went on to lose the game, 31-12.

Afterward, Nehlen said, "We knew going in, that Florida State had better speed than we did. But, so did Florida last year in the Peach Bowl. In looking at the films of Florida State, I didn't think they were a better team than we were. Our special teams broke down. We gave up a 95-yard kickoff return for a touchdown. Our kicking game broke down. We had a field goal and punt blocked. We had things happen to us that hadn't all season.

"The steady rain hurt our passing attack, but that's no alibi. It rained on Florida State, too, and I noticed their quarterback had no trouble throwing the ball.

"The only consolation is that we got to our second consecutive bowl. There are a lot of teams in the country that would have loved to have traded places with us."

Following the Gator Bowl defeat, the same Orlando sports columnist, who wrote that WVU didn't belong in the Peach Bowl against Florida, took another shot at Nehlen, the Mountaineers and their fans. He wrote, "Maybe Nehlen is one of those coaches who comprehends only X's and O's and quotes by eminent philosophers like Mean Joe Greene and Jethro Bodine", and he called WVU followers "Fans who pack innertubes and beach towels in their pickup trucks."

Nehlen dismissed the slam at his program and WVU's fans. He was disappointed over the loss, but proud of his team's second consecutive 9-3 season and second straight finish in the final top 20 polls. WVU was voted 19th by both wire services.

"Was losing the Gator Bowl my fault?" asked Nehlen. "Well, I was the head coach. Sure, it was my fault. I'm the boss. Obviously, we were in Florida too long and the team went stale. And obviously, if I had to do it over, I would change a few things. But at the time, I thought what we were doing was the best way to prepare.

"How was I to know my kids weren't going to get after Florida State? How did I know that they would peak two days before the game and then get bored? How did I know some of my young pups would let down? Honest to golly, if I had known all that, I'd be the smartest coach in America.

"I've always said we all learn from experiences, and that win, lose, or draw, you always come away a little bit smarter. I learned that the next bowl we go to, we're going to go down about three or four days in advance, have about three practices, and then tee it up.

"All the rest of that stuff — fancy hotels, nice side trips, great food, etc., it's a bunch of malarky."

Chapter Fourteen

1983.

It was the season of the murderers' row, the goal-line stand, the top 10 ranking, the standing-room-only crowds and the television appearances. And it was the year Don Nehlen's 'Sleeping Giant' awakened and made football fans across the nation sit up and take notice.

Nehlen's fourth season as head coach of the West Virginia University Mountaineers began like no other in WVU history.

Two-and-a-half weeks before the opening game at Mountaineer Field on Sept. 3, against Ohio University, Nehlen paced the new 145-yard grass practice field on the plateau in front of the WVU facilities building and watched his squad go through the morning session of a two-a-day practice. Nehlen is never still. Always on the move.

It promised to be a scorching mid-August day. But Nehlen said, "It won't be as hot on this grass as it would have been inside the stadium on the AstroTurf. And the natural turf will be easier on the players' legs. We don't need a bunch of guys going around with pulled muscles, or tired legs. We have too much work to do."

He already had the problem of interruptions. And those who know Nehlen know he doesn't like anything to bother his concentration once pre-season drills start. But he was resigned to the fact that interruptions "went with the new territory."

That new territory was success. Nehlen's reputation was growing by leaps and bounds. After the Gator Bowl appearance in December 1982, Nehlen, along with Florida coach Charlie Pell, was picked to be an assistant coach on Texas A&M coach Jackie Sherrill's Hula Bowl staff.

It was a nice trip," was all Nehlen had to say about that prestigious honor.

Now, a CBS-TV crew was coming to Morgantown to film a segment on the Mountaineers' camp to be aired with segments on Tennessee, Auburn and Washington on a '1983 College Football Kickoff' special.

Nehlen said, "The interruptions are a nuisance, because we've got so much work to do. However, we have to be delighted. At least, the network people know we're here. It seems everybody wants to know about our team now. I don't know what we've done to get all this attention. Golly dang, my first season here we were 6-6 and were terrible. But after that, I guess we probably surprised a few folks."

Surprised wasn't the word. His record spoke for itself — two 9-3 seasons, two bowl appearances and two finishes in the top 20 polls.

Interest in the West Virginia Mountaineers was at an all-time high. Season ticket sales for the '83 season were expected to reach 30,000. The Mountaineers were picked 15th in pre-season polls by Street & Smith and Playboy magazines. In other polls WVU was a consensus No. 23 pick.

Quarterback Jeff Hostetler, the Penn State transfer, was now a senior and mentioned as a possible Heisman Trophy candidate. "In building a team," said Nehlen, "you have to start with a quarterback. We feel we have a pretty good one."

Nehlen added, "and my man Woody is back, too." The coach referred to junior field goal kicker Paul Woodside, who set three NCAA records and shattered the Mountaineers' career field goal record in 1982. Woodside made 28 of 31 field goal attempts and was 23-for-23 from inside 40 yards.

Television crews, radio interviews and hordes of sportswriters weren't the only interruptions in Nehlen's work schedule. There was a brief interruption involving a player, one who decided to turn in his uniform. It was Scott Lowery, a promising sophomore from Griffithsville, W. Va., who felt called to exchange his football gear for a Bible and transfer from WVU to Appalachian Bible College.

Lowery met with Nehlen in the coach's office and told Nehlen of his decision, and then cried. Nehlen shed a few tears, too.

Afterward, Nehlen said, "I hated to see Scott go, because he would have been a fine football player. But he said he felt called to do God's work. He was excited about going, but sad about leaving. I understood. Hey, my kids are young men with serious decisions to make about their lives. I told Scott my door would always be open to him.

"I love that kid. And I told him, 'You stay in touch with me, you hear?'

"Gee, you build so many beautiful relationships in this business. And that's the important part about it. Football plays only a small part."

The Mountaineers were bigger and stronger as the '83 season approached, the result of more than a few hours in the weight room in the off-season. Forty-two of Nehlen's players weighed 235 pounds or more. Twenty-one of those 42 weighed 250 or more. And all bench pressed 350 pounds or more. "We're stronger," said Nehlen, "But we're not strong enough. I doubt that we'll ever be strong enough to suit me.

"But I will admit that strengthwise, this year's team is the strongest I've had since I've been here. We have pretty good size up front, and have more second-stringers and third-stringers who weigh 245 to 250 pounds. However, when I see the size of some of the teams around the country, it seems like we're small. I mean, there is Ohio State, which averages about 265 pounds up front. Southern Methodist averages about 285 pounds. I don't know what we average. Maybe 250 or 255.

"The good thing is we're starting to get the size where we can play the Pitts and the Penn States. We weren't able to do that my first two years here. Last year we started getting there and could pretty much slug it out with anybody. Maybe we'll be able to do that this year."

In 1982, the Mountaineers were faced with an enormous task in their season opener — to play Oklahoma at Oklahoma.

"Our kids were scared to death this time last year," said Nehlen. "Even some of my coaches were squirming around. But we went to Oklahoma and got the job done (a 41-27 win). Now, this year we're opening with another O.U. But it's Ohio University, not Oklahoma University."

And since it was Ohio U., instead of Oklahoma U., Nehlen knew West Virginia fans expected the Mountaineers to open with a one-sided victory. But he didn't see it that way. Ohio U was in the Mid-American Conference, and Nehlen used to coach in that conference. He knew all about Ohio U.

"Don't tell me they can't beat us," he said, "because they can. We're not going to go out there, throw our helmets on the field and walk off with a victory."

Nehlen was wrong, because that's just what his team did. To the delight of an overflow Mountaineer Field crowd of 54,612, the Mountaineers romped to a 55-3 win.

After the first possession of the second half, WVU led, 34-3, and Nehlen put in his second team. West Virginia rolled up 479 yards in total offense and limited the Bobcats to 153 yards. Hostetler played only half the game and completed 15 of 23 passes for 205 yards and one touchdown, a 38-yard toss to wide receiver Gary Mullen. Woodside booted two field goals.

There was no question in the minds of the WVU faithful that the Mountaineers could have named the score against Ohio U. "We certainly didn't try to score 55 points," said Nehlen. "In the fourth quarter, we didn't try to throw the ball at all. All we did was run it. I guess I overestimated Ohio University.

"But there's one good thing about winning the first game. Now, no matter what happens, we can't lose them all."

The second game was against College of Pacific's Tigers, another team that Nehlen feared might surprise the Mountaineers if they took them lightly. Again, his fears were unfounded.

A second consecutive overflow home crowd (54,581) turned out to watch West Virginia roll to a 48-7 win. The Mountaineers had 429 yards total offense. And again, Nehlen's starters played only about half the game.

Hostetler was 15 for 24 for 213 yards and two touchdowns, and Woodside kicked two more field goals.

In the equivalent of one full game (one half against Ohio U. and one half against Pacific), Hostetler completed 30 of 47 passes for 418 yards and three TDs. Fans were excited about the quarterback they had nicknamed 'Hoss'.

The Mountaineers were averaging 52.5 points a game and had scored more points than any other WVU team had ever scored in the first two games. They were No. 1 in the nation in total defense, No. 9 in total offense and No. 2 in scoring.

"Pacific was a little better than Ohio U.," said Nehlen. "I know, we're 2-0, but both wins came so easily that it's difficult to tell just how daggoned good we are. The two big things I've noticed are that this team is confident and believes it can win.

"Now, we have to go to Maryland. We've sorta had their number the last two years. Maryland is big, strong and fast. They played in the Hula Bowl last year and lost to a very good Washington team, 21-20. However, I don't feel they're any better than we are. The thing we have to hope for when we go to Maryland is that our defense plays like the devil.

"I can't wait to tee it up against Maryland and see how good we are. I love it. This Maryland game has me jumping up and down."

Nehlen was excited. Not only was it a big game against an undefeated top 20 team, but the game had been moved to night and would be televised on national cable by WTBS. Including the two national television appearances in the bowls the last two years, it would be WVU's sixth television appearance in the last 14 games. Prior to that, it had taken the Mountaineers 12 years to get six television appearances.

Maryland Coach Bobby Ross, whose Terrapins lost to WVU by the grand total of five points the last two seasons, said of the Mountaineers, "You don't accomplish what they've accomplished unless you are able to outslug, outhit and outplay people. From what I've seen on film, Don Nehlen has his team playing with tremendous emotion. I love to see that in a football team."

The 14th-ranked Mountaineers clashed with 19th-ranked Maryland before another overflow crowd. This time it was a throng of 54,715 at Byrd Stadium in College Park, Md., and was the first game of six that Nehlen described as "our murderers' row."

The Mountaineers' murderers' row included Maryland, Boston College at Boston, Pitt at Mountaineer Field, Virginia Tech at Mountaineer Field, Penn State at State College, Pa., and Miami, Fla., in Miami.

"I don't think any West Virginia team has ever been called upon to do what this one has to do," said Nehlen. "Holy criminy, those teams are murder! All are in the top 20. And four of those games are on the road. Make no mistake, the picnic is over. We're into the meat of our schedule. I just hope it's not the meat grinder."

The opening minutes of the Maryland game were disastrous for the Mountaineers. West Virginia, a team that had led the nation in turnover margin the year before, turned the ball over on its first two possessions when the Terrapins picked off two Hostetler passes. After six minutes of play, WVU trailed, 10-0.

Nehlen wasn't concerned. He said, "We tell our kids to never look at the scoreboard. I don't, either. The only thing I was concerned about was our mistakes. I'm sure our fans thought things looked bad. But I started to see our defense play with more zest and zingo. When I saw that, I felt we had a great chance to get back in the game, despite the mistakes.

"I always tell my kids to never worry about mistakes, because they are better than that. And when a kid does make a mistake, I say, 'Don't worry about it. Forget it.' I've learned that when a player expects to fail, he'll live up to his expectations. We don't coach mistakes."

The Mountaineers battled back. Woodside kicked a 45-yard field goal, one that Nehlen described as "a thing of beauty." And near the end of the half, WVU safety Tim Agee intercepted a pass at the Maryland 17 and returned the ball to the 14. Two plays later, fullback Ron Wolfley scored on a two-yard plunge, and the game was tied, 10-10.

In the third quarter, West Virginia scored twice. Sophomore tailback Tommy Gray scored on a 17-yard run, and Hostetler teamed with tight end Rob Bennett on a 42-yard TD pass. The Mountaineers were in command, 24-10. The final TD, which sealed the victory, came with five minutes to play when Hostetler hit Rich Hollins in the end zone with a 43-yard toss. WVU led, 31-13, and went on to win, 31-21.

After that third straight victory, the Mountaineers jumped into the top 10. United Press International's coaches' poll committee voted WVU No. 8. Nehlen, who was on the UPI committee, picked his team 12th, the position The Associated Press poll had the Mountaineers.

After the win, Nehlen said, "You don't have any idea what a tough place Maryland is to play at. We had a lot to overcome tonight. First, our bus driver got lost on the way to the stadium. I was about to have kittens. We barely made it in time to warm up. That driver must have been a big Maryland fan.

"But when we came back from that 10-0 deficit and walked off at the half all even, I told my kids, 'Hey, men, if we eliminate the big enemy, which is us, we'll have no problem. All we have to do is put some points on the board and turn it over to the defense.'

"One thing I always tell my kids when we go into a big game, especially a big one away from home, is that they are going to win the game at some point, lose it at some point, win it again, lose it again and win it again. And I tell them all they have to do is keep the faith.

"I don't know if we were stronger than Maryland, but I know Maryland wasn't stronger than we were. My first year here they bounced us around like rubber balls. The second year they bounced us around a couple of times. Last year they bounced us once.

"This year we bounced a few of their guys.

"And the great thing about the game of football is that we proved we were a good team against Maryland. Now, we had to go to Boston College the next game and prove it all over again."

For the second consecutive Saturday, the Mountaineers tackled a top 20 team. Boston College was ranked 15th. And, for the second week in a row, the Mountaineers' game was to be televised. ABC-TV announced early that week the game would be on regional television.

Boston College had a dangerous offense, led by junior quarterback Doug Flutie, a scrambler in the Fran Tarkenton mold who was Heisman Trophy material. Eagles' coach Jack Bicknell said of his team, "We're not too bad. I know West Virginia will be a slight favorite. But with Flutie running our attack, we're explosive."

Boston College was sixth in the nation in scoring, averaging 39.3 points. WVU was fourth, averaging 44.7.

The Mountaineers, gunning for their fourth straight win, barely made it to the stadium on time this week, too. This time the bus carrying them from the hotel to the field was involved in a wreck. "I just hoped that wasn't an omen of things to come," said Nehlen.

It wasn't. West Virginia swarmed and surprised the Eagles on the opening kickoff. Boston College won the toss and elected to receive. Paul Woodside kicked off, and the Eagles' star runner, Troy Stratford, took the ball on his five and started up the field.

WVU freshman lineback West Turner, half-brother of former Mountaineer All-American Jim Braxton, charged downfield under a full head of steam. It was 'the hit' of the game. Turner barreled into Stratford at the 15-yard line, separated him from the ball and put him out of the game with an injured knee. WVU's Cam Zopp recovered and the Mountaineers had possession at the Boston College 16.

Three plays later, Hostetler passed four yards over the middle to Tommy Gray for a touchdown. Eighty-seven seconds had ticked off the clock and WVU led, 7-0.

The Mountaineers' next drive stalled, and they lined up in punt formation from their own 33. Boston College was determined to block the punt and lined up all but two players on one side of the ball.

West Virginia fullback Ron Wolfley, the up blocking back on punts, spotted the gaping hole on the right side of the Eagles' line and signaled for a fake punt. The snap went to Wolfley, and he surprised everyone by going untouched 67 yards for a touchdown. Three more minutes had ticked off, and the Mountaineers led, 14-0.

"I always give my punting team the option of calling the fake," Nehlen said. "Wolfley saw that Boston College had only two men lined up on one side of the ball. We're not going to let anyone do that to us. Now, my kids have to use commonsense. I'm not going to let them call it all the time and get us killed."

Wolfley explained, "It was my call. I didn't know whether I was going to be a hero or a goat. I was sure I could at least get the first down, but never dreamed I'd go all the way."

Midway in the second quarter, the Mountaineers surprised Boston College again. This time WVU had possession at the Boston College 15-yard line. It was third and 13. Hostetler handed off to flanker Gary Mullen on a flanker-around play. Mullen strolled into the end zone. The lead was now 24-3.

After that quick start, West Virginia went on to win, 27-17.

Despite Turner's big hit, Wolfley's fake punt call and Mullens' flanker-around, the big surprise of the game was turned in by the West Virginia defense. In the first quarter, Boston College had a first down and goal to go at the WVU five-yard line.

On first down, an off-tackle play netted one yard.

On second down, the Mountaineers were called for pass interference. The penalty was half the distance to the goal and a first down. Now the Eagles had first and goal to go from the WVU two.

On first down, a fullback plunge off the left side netted one yard.

Two more cracks at the heart of the WVU defense were stopped cold. Now, it was fourth down, and Boston's College's fifth attempt to score.

The Eagles tried the Mountaineers' middle again, and were thrown back for a one-yard loss.

Boston College tried five times to score from the five-yard line and came away with only three yards and no points.

And West Virginia added insult to injury by taking the ball and marching 73 yards to the Boston College 25. From there Paul Woodside kicked a 41-yard field goal.

Near the end of the third quarter, with the Mountaineers holding a 27-10 lead, Boston College had the ball in the shadow of the WVU goal again. This time the Eagles were at the three-yard line with first and goal. Four plays netted minus one yard, and the Mountaineers took over at the four.

In nine plays near the WVU goal, Boston College netted just two yards.

"Those were two dynamite efforts by our defense," said Nehlen. "Just dynamite! Imagine, Boston College had 10 cracks at us inside our five-yard line and came away empty-handed. It's a good thing, too, because that Flutie almost drove us crazy trying to chase him."

Flutie threw 53 passes and completed 23 for 418 yards, but had three intercepted. He scrambled nine times for 46 yards.

During the post-game interview, Nehlen asked a Boston writer, "Is Flutie just a junior?"

When informed Flutie was, Nehlen moaned, "Oh, Lord, you mean we've got to face him again next year? Criminy, he'll run that same play where he fakes and keeps the ball and rolls out on that naked reverse. And our guys will still end up chasing the guy without the ball."

"Oh, well, we'll worry about that next year. The biggest thing about this win was that for the second week in a row we were able to go into enemy territory, play a good football team and win. And we won today despite the fact that I thought our team played only an average game.

"We got ahead of them early, and after that there was no way we were going to throw up the middle or down the sideline. We were going to do what we knew we could do and make Boston College beat us. We weren't going to beat ourselves.

"We expect our defense to play well. But, golly sakes, didn't those guys make some great plays?"

Boston College and Flutie had riddled the Mountaineers' defense for 29 first downs and 505 yards total offense. It was most yardage ever gained against a Nehlen-coached WVU team. But although the West Virginia defense bent, it didn't break. Twice the Eagles were so close to the WVU goal that if WVU had been guilty of an infraction, the referees couldn't have moved the ball.

In spite of it all, the Mountaineers were now 4-0 and solidly entrenched among the nation's elite teams. They were ranked sixth in the country by UPI and seventh by AP.

And West Virginia was one-third of the way through murderers' row.

Next was arch-rival Pitt.

Life was not kind to Coach Nehlen at Bowling Green University.

"You gotta be kidding!"

"You guys want the blocking sled to win?"

Fullback Eddie Hill listens intently.

"They were that close to the goal line."

Victory can be sweet. Coach Nehlen hugs Calvin Turner in jubilation.

Athletic Director Fred Schaus and Coach Nehlen are all smiles when Art Gregory extends an invitation to play in the Peach Bowl.

The coach's mother, Marge, at her home in Canton, Ohio.

Chapter Fifteen

For West Virginia Mountaineer football fans, there is one thing better than a 90-yard winning touchdown drive.

It's a 90-yard winning touchdown drive — AGAINST PITT!

On Oct. 1, 1983, all the Mountaineer Field seats were filled. Fans were sitting in the aisles. The temporary end zone bleachers were filled. Fans were sitting on the bank and lining the walkway beneath the scoreboard. There was even a standing-room-only crowd in the press box. An all-time record crowd of 64,076 was on hand to witness the backyard brawl between the two old rivals.

West Virginia vs. Pitt.

Don Nehlen kept insisting it was "just another game," the fifth game on his Mountaineers schedule.

It was not just another game. It was 'THE' game. To say it was just another game was like saying World War II was just another war, that the landing on the moon was just another shot in space, that the polio vaccine was just another medical discovery, that open-heart surgery was just another operation.

This was the 76th meeting between the two teams. The Mountaineers hadn't beaten the Panthers since 1975, when Bill McKenzie kicked a last-second field goal in a 17-14 thriller. And Nehlen's first three WVU teams had lost to Pitt by scores of 42-14, 17-0 and 16-13.

Pitt came into the game with a 2-1 record and a No. 20 ranking in the polls. It hadn't given up a touchdown on the ground, and had the No. 1 defense in the nation. Despite these statistics, the Mountaineers were favored, by anywhere from six to 10 points. Why not? West Virginia was 4-0, ranked No. 6 and No. 7 in the wire service polls and already drawing the attention of bowl scouts.

CBS-TV was going to regionally televise the game (WVU's third consecutive TV appearance). Scouts from the Orange Bowl would be in attendance, and they wouldn't be there to look at Pitt.

There was no way it could be just another game. And while Nehlen talked that way, he didn't act that way. He closed WVU practices. "I did it for one reason only," he said. "There are so many distractions around here. The students are going crazy. Everybody wants to interview the players. Our kids need to concentrate, because on Saturday we want to go out on that field and show off what we have going here at West Virginia."

Nehlen admitted there were real "plums" at stake.

"A victory over Pitt is important for all the obvious reasons," he said. "It will keep us undefeated. It will ensure that we stay in the top 10. It will help us in recruiting this winter when we go into western Pennsylvania. And it will certainly make everyone in college football aware that West Virginia is out there. Pitt has had the national image because of its success and exposure on television.

"Now we are on the verge of getting the same thing. That's why this game is so important."

It was a warm, overcast day. The temperature was 70 degrees. A perfect day for the battle. Pitt won the toss and elected to receive. The crowd let go with a deafening roar as Steve Superick kicked off. The game was under way.

The Mountaineers, although minus the services of top runner Tommy Gray, who was sidelined with an injured knee, wasted no time getting after the Panthers. Pitt managed only two yards in three downs and had to punt. It was a short punt, and West Virginia had possession at the Pitt 42.

West Virginia went to the air on the first play, and quarterback Jeff Hostetler passed 26 yards to tight end Rob Bennett. Tailback King Harvey ran for two yards, and fullback Ron Wolfley ran for eight more. Then Hostetler passed 19 yards to wide receiver Wayne Brown for the touchdown. WVU led, 7-0.

Pitt tied it with a 'fluke' touchdown minutes later. Hostetler dropped back to pass, was hit, and the ball popped out of his hands. Pitt's Bill Maas grabbed the ball out of the air and went 75 yards to score.

WVU was forced to punt on its next possession. The Mountaineers covered the punt and thought the officials had blown it dead at the Pitt 36. They hadn't and Pitt's Tom Flynn picked the ball up and ran it to the WVU 28. Two plays later, Pitt had scored again to take a 14-7 lead.

Nehlen muttered, "Holy criminy, mistakes, mistakes, mistakes. Boy we're really stinking up the place."

But he told his players the same thing he always did when things were going bad, "Don't look at the scoreboard, and forget about the mistakes. Mistakes are accidents. The heck with them. Don't worry about them. Just go on to the next play."

Nehlen added, "I saw a few of you guys losing your cool out there in the first half. Let me tell you something, if you swing at somebody, you're out of the game. And if the refs don't throw you out, I will. Millions of people are watching us. Let's go get 'em."

The Mountaineers scored their second touchdown on the third play of the second quarter to tie the score after receiving a fumbled punt at the Pitt 25. Harvey got the TD on a one-yard plunge. But the Panthers went ahead again with a 35-yard touchdown pass when they caught the WVU secondary flatfooted. Pitt led, 21-14, at halftime.

In the locker room, Nehlen said, "We are OK. All we have to do is eliminate our mistakes. They got two touchdowns on flukes. They're not going to beat us on fluke plays. Let's go get 'em."

A 49-yard field goal by Paul Woodside cut WVU's deficit to 21-17 after three quarters. And the stage was set for the final, frantic 15 minutes.

With 12:27 to go in the game, the Mountaineers forced Pitt to punt, and Willie Drewrey returned the ball to the 20. However, West Virginia was called for clipping on the play and penalized to the 10.

The Mountaineers were deep in their own territory with nearly the length of the field separating them from the Pitt goal. Nehlen knew the chances of mounting a 90-yard drive against Pitt's fine defense were slim. But that's exactly what WVU did.

The Mountaineers marched 90 yards in 14 plays, 13 of them running plays, to score the winning touchdown. Wolfley carried four times in the drive and gained 31 yards, and freshman back Pat Randolph carried four times and gained 24 yards. Hostetler ran the ball over the goal line from six yards out on a bootleg play. The record crowd of 64,076 rocked the stadium with an ear-splitting roar.

West Virginia had taken the lead, 24-21. Six minutes, 22 seconds remained in the game. At this point, the Mountaineers' defense took over and intercepted passes on Pitt's final two possessions.

The game was over. Nehlen Mountaineers were 5-0. They had beaten Pitt, and did it in front of a record crowd, in front of Orange Bowl scouts, in front of a regional television audience. And they had scored 24 points against a team that had come into the game boasting the No. 1 defense in the country.

Nehlen said, "Our kids simply hitched up their belts on that last drive and rammed the ball down Pitt's throat. That was one of the finest touchdown drives you'll ever see, and it was a great exhibition of the character of our team. There aren't very many teams in the country that can march 90 yards, mostly on the ground, against Pitt. It was a great, great win. Now, maybe we'll get some respect."

How about No. 4 in the national polls? That's where the Mountaineers were voted after the impressive come-back against the Panthers. And one poll, based on a mathematical formula by Penn State mathematics professor and published by *USA Today*, actually had West Virginia as the nation's No. 1 team.

I'm tickled to death to be ranked No. 4 in the polls," said Nehlen. "I'd rather be ranked than not ranked. It's a great feeling to know our program is finally being recognized. But I'm more pleased that we have an open date next. That will give us time to rest and let our bumps and bruises heal.

"Do you realize, we have played three top 20 teams in a row, and played two of them on the road, and won all three? We're halfway through murderer's row.

"I just hope we don't lose our momentum, because we can't afford to stumble. Our program isn't established

yet. If we lose, we could go from chicken salad to you-know-what in a hurry."

After the week off, West Virginia resumed by entertaining Virginia Tech. And believe it or not, the Mountaineers' game was to be regionally televised again — by CBS-TV. This would be the Mountaineers' fourth TV appearance in as many games.

Nehlen said, "It's nice, but we can't lose sight of our goals. We're getting a lot of attention, but if we're not careful we could wind up with our minds on all that stuff — and not on football.

"People are calling from all over the country wanting to interview my players. I don't get too bent out of shape about that. Now, I don't want anyone talking to them after Wednesday. Then that becomes a distraction. But I'm not going to tell my kids they can't talk to television, radio and newspaper people. That's part of growing up."

Virginia Tech came into Mountaineer Field with a 4-1 record and confident it could end West Virginia's winning streak. It was the Hokies' chance to gain top 20 recognition. It was a chance to beat a nationally ranked team. Tech coach Bill Dooley said, "We feel sure a victory over West Virginia would put us in the top 20. After all, we have the No. 2 defense in the country and are No. 2 in points allowed. Our goal this season was to go 10-1, and since we've already lost that one, this game is very important to us."

Meanwhile, Nehlen was hoping his team's momentum was still present. He knew his Mountaineers had played with great emotion and intensity in the first five games and couldn't afford to lose that edge.

For the fourth straight home game, Mountaineer Field was filled to overflowing (57,181) when the Mountaineers took to the artificial turf against Virginia Tech. And Nehlen's fears about his team losing momentum weren't unfounded. West Virginia put on a lackluster offensive performance.

The Mountaineers recovered a fumble at the Tech 23, couldn't move the ball and settled for a Woodside field goal. But Woodside was roughed on the play and West Virginia took the penalty and a first down. The Mountaineers scored a touchdown four plays later on a one-yard sneak by Hostetler. West Virginia held a 7-0 lead.

The only other WVU scores were two field goals by Woodside.

Fortunately, the Mountaineers defense came up with another outstanding performance and held the Hokies to 112 yards rushing, 109 yards passng, and no points.

West Virginia had its sixth straight win, 13-0.

"We fumbled at the Virginia Tech one, threw an interception in the end zone and had a 77-yard punt return for a touchdown call back," muttered Nehlen. "Take those three plays and put them in the plus column, and we have 21 more points on the board and a pretty big win. That's not bad against a team that had the No. 2 defense in the nation coming into the game. And I'll take a shutout anytime we can get one.

"We didn't play with a lot of emotion against Virginia Tech, and that bothers me. Our team was kind of workmanlike in this game. Maybe it's a good sign, I don't know. I do know we were good enough to win. Maybe the players were saving their emotion for our next game. I hope so.''

West Virginia was now 6-0 and two-thirds of the way through murderers' row. But the game was at Penn State.

Nehlen exclaimed, ''Wow! Now we go to Penn State. The big one is coming up. But it's just another big one. They're all big at this point in the season. When you get 6-0 and in the top 10, do you think you're going to have any easy games?''

Nehlen knew the Nittany Lions were defending national champs and had been having a few problems in '83. Penn State, in one of the worst starts ever for a Joe Paterno-coached team, had lost three of its first seven games. But Nehlen knew, too, that Penn State had beaten Alabama when Alabama was No. 3 in the country. And he knew Penn State would be ''primed and ready'' for his Mountaineers that Saturday in Beaver Stadium.

''Penn State is a very, very good football team,'' said Nehlen. ''Exactly why they haven't been blowing people out, I don't know. Maybe there's a chemistry missing. But I guarantee you one thing: Joe Paterno will have his kids breathing fire when we take the field against them.

''But we're 6-0, and one poll (*USA Today/Cable News Network* poll) has us No. 3 in the country behind Nebraska and Texas. You can bet our kids will be flying all over the place against Penn State. They'd better be, or we're going to be in for a long afternoon.''

West Virginia hadn't beaten Penn State since 1955. One sportswriter wrote, ''A cup of coffee was a nickel, oranges were two cents each and sirloin steak was 65 cents a pound the last time the Mountaineers beat the Nittany Lions. But I have a hunch Penn State's domination of West Virginia will end this Saturday on the field at the base of Mount Nittany.''

Experts thought so, too, because they had the Mountaineers favored.

They were all wrong. An all-time record Penn State crowd of 83,307 turned out on a cloudy Oct. 23 afternoon and watched as the Nittany Lions played a flawless first half to lead, 21-10. Quarterback Doug Strang completed 12 of 14 passes, two of them for touchdowns, and scored once himself on a one-yard run.

The Mountaineers tried valiantly to come back in the second half. They scored early in the third quarter on a two-yard pass from Jeff Hostetler to Pat Randolph to narrow the gap to 21-17. And after Penn State put 10 more points on the board, Woodside kicked a 26-yard field goal to cut the deficit to 31-20 at the end of the third quarter. On the play before the field goal, Randolph caught a pass in the end zone from Hostetler, but WVU was called for ''an illegal pick'' on the play.

''Now, we surprise them with an onside kick,'' said Nehlen.

The Mountaineers did and recovered the ball at the Penn State 49. But in eight plays they moved the ball only 22 yards and had to settle for another Woodside field goal — a 43-yarder. West Virginia was within eight points of the Lions, 31-23.

Penn State fumbled the ensuing kickoff but recovered the ball, and the Nittany Lions put the game away minutes later when freshman running back D.J. Dozier scored on a screen pass from Strang. The play covered 46 yards. Penn State led, 38-23, and went on to win, 41-23. When the final gun sounded, Penn State fans tore down the goal posts to celebrate the 25th consecutive victory over West Virginia.

Nehlen said, ''Well, I guess we've earned Penn State's respect. It's the first time they ever tore down the goal posts after beating us.

''To make a long story short, we couldn't stop 'em. They just went up and down the field. Every time we'd get close — boom! They'd score again. I think our defense must have missed 30 tackles. And those missed tackles resulted in Penn State runners gaining something like 170 yards after we hit 'em. When you're in a big game like this and your defense doesn't play well, you have no chance of winning. It was disappointing that our defense didn't play with great emotion.

''But we're still 6-1. There aren't very many teams in America that could play the schedule we've played and be 6-1. What we have to do now is profit from this loss.''

As a result of the first defeat, the Mountaineers tumbled out of the top 10. They were 12th in the AP poll and 13th in the UPI poll.

A trip to Miami, Fla., to play the University of Miami Hurricanes in the Organge Bowl was next. It was the final game of the six-game stretch that Nehlen called murderers' row.

Nehlen had an assistant coach scout Miami and ''the scouting report was bad.''

''First of all, Miami is 7-1 and rated No. 7 in the country,'' Nehlen said. ''They have great team speed and a heckuva quarterback in red-shirt freshman Bernie Kosar. We know all about Kosar because we tried to recruit him. Miami will be at its best for us. We always seem to catch teams at their best.''

Miami coach Howard Schnellenberger minced no words. He said, ''West Virginia is a good team, probably better than any we've played. They are certainly better than Notre Dame (Miami beat Notre Dame, 20-0). But we have a very talented football team. We're not concerned about playing West Virginia. We're concerned about going 10-1 and getting a berth in the Orange Bowl.''

The strength of the Miami football team surprised Nehlen. ''We knew they were fast, but we didn't think they'd be that strong,'' he said after his Mountaineers suffered a 20-3 defeat.

In the opening minutes of the game, it appeared the Mountaineers would have no trouble moving the ball against the Hurricanes. They took the opening kickoff and marched 75 yards to the Miami five. There the Miami defense stiffened, and Woodside came in to boot a 21-yard field goal.

After that, it was all Miami. West Virginia was held to two yards rushing. ''I can't remember a team of mine ever being held to two yards rushing,'' moaned Nehlen. ''I didn't think anybody could do that to us.'' Miami went on to win the national championship by beating Nebraska, 31-30, in the Orange Bowl.

The Mountaineers had suffered their second straight defeat. Their record was now 6-2, and they tumbled to 17th and 20th in the polls.

Nehlen said, "This was the last of our six tough games. Between me, you and the gatepost, I prayed we would be 3-3 after those murderous games. And we came through it 4-2. Now, we have a chance to win eight or nine games on the season. That will get us another bowl and be a heckuva year.

"I know our fans are disappointed that we lost two in a row. But we lost two games to two great football teams. The Mountaineers are still alive and kicking. Our kids aren't going to fall over and die. We're still 18th in the nation in total defense. And we're still shooting for a great season."

West Virginia returned to Mountaineer Field to play Temple. Scouts from the Citrus, Peach and Hall of Fame bowls were on hand. A capacity crowd of 50,514 was on hand, too. The Mountaineers didn't disappoint the scouts or the fans as they rolled up a 24-3 halftime lead and coasted to a 27-9 victory. The win moved WVU up to 15th in both wire service polls.

Afterward, Nehlen said, "Now we hold our own destiny. If we win next week against Rutgers, that will give us eight wins and we'll go to a bowl. Eight wins separates you from a lot of folks.

The bowl rumors flew in earnest. It was certain that an 8-2 record, although there was still a season finale against Syracuse in the Syracuse Carrier Dome, would get the Mountaineers their third straight bowl bid. Two days after the Rutgers win, the 'unofficial' word was out. West Virginia would be going to the Dec. 22 Hall of Fame in Birmingham, Ala. The opponent would be the winner of the upcoming Kentucky-Tennessee game.

University President E. Gordon Gee announced that the school passed up possible opportunities to go the Citrus and Peach bowls. Gee said that the date of the Citrus Bowl in Orlando, Fla., was Dec. 17 and "presented a difficult problem" for WVU's final exams. He added that the team elected to not go back to the Peach Bowl since it had been there in 1981.

Several WVU players expressed displeasure that they were going to the Hall of Fame Bowl and called the university's bowl selection process "pitiful." The players' first choice of bowls had been the Citrus Bowl.

Nehlen said, "The Hall of Fame Bowl is an up-and-coming bowl. Hey, we didn't have that many choices! The date of the Citrus Bowl interfered with our final exams. And after all, our kids are in school to get educations. We didn't want to go back to the Peach Bowl or Gator bowls. We wanted to go to a bowl we hadn't been to before.

"And after we lost those games to Penn State and Miami, we were out of the major bowl picture. But I'll tell you this, we would have accepted a bowl bid if we'd had to take the 'Alaska Bowl.' I know some of our kids are a little disappointed in the bowl we're going to. That's crap. A lot of teams would like to trade places with us.

"Now, we have to forget this bowl talk and get prepared for Syracuse. We have to play them in that Carrier Dome and noise is a great problem there. But we don't want to have the same thing happen this year that happened to us up there in 1981." That was when WVU lost to the Orangemen, 27-24, after already having the Peach Bowl bid. Now, the Mountaineers 'unofficially' had the Hall of Fame Bowl bid. "We don't want to stumble again," added Nehlen.

The game was to regionally televised by CBS-TV. The coverage by CBS, plus the upcoming bowl game, would give the Mountaineers six television appearances in one season, resulting in extra income of nearly $2 million. Also, it would be WVU's 11th television appearance, including bowls, since Nehlen had arrived on the scene.

West Virginia had had only 11 televison appearances in history before Nehlen.

The Mountaineers, 14th in one poll and 15th in the other, invaded the Carrier Dome determined to end the regular season on a winning note. Syracuse was 5-5 and equally determined to win, because a victory would give the Orangemen their first winning season in three years under Coach Dick MacPherson.

Syracuse did it again. The Orangemen spoiled the Mountaineers' post-game bowl celebration by beating WVU, 27-16. Nehlen was uphappy that his team didn't "display any spark." He said, "I don't think I believe in superstitions, but I'm not so sure after what happened to us up here again. We made so many mistakes it boggled my mind. We had 14 penalties. Once, we got inside Syracuse's four-yard line and had three straight penalties. That's not like us. We screwed up every time we had an opportunity to win this game"

Nehlen also voiced displeasure at the noise in the Carrier Dome. "This dome is going to be a real problem," he said. "It's the toughest place in the country to play. And just wait until Syracuse gets its program going. The crowd noise just bounces back and forth off the walls. The noise seems to come from everywhere. This the first game I've ever coached where my quarterback wasn't about to call audibles at the line of scrimmage one time. That just took about 40 percent of our offense away from us. I don't know, maybe when you play in the dome you'll just have to tell your quarterback not to take the snap until the crowd quites down. I don't know how an official can make kids play when they can't hear. And when Syracuse has the ball, it's so quiet you can here a pin drop. The Carrier Dome is just murder."

In the locker room after the loss, Charles Martin, head of the Hall of Fame Bowl committee, officially extended West Virginia the bowl bid. The Mountaineers would play Kentucky, another loser that day (10-0 to Tennessee).

Nehlen and his players tried to act excited, but their hearts weren't in it. The loss to the Orangemen left a sour taste in the Mountaineers' mouths. "I'm not making excuses," said Nehlen, "because we played like horse manure. But I'm not too sure it wouldn't be better if the bowls waited an extra week before making their selections.

You have no idea how difficult it is to play on the road when you have a bowl bid wrapped up. There are so many distractions, not to mention an opponent just waiting and itching to upset you.''

West Virginia ended the 11-game schedule 8-3 and was 18th in the AP poll and 19th in the UPI poll. Four teams the Mountaineers had defeated — Pitt, Boston College, Maryland and Virginia Tech — were ranked ahead of them in the UPI poll, and three teams they had defeated — Pitt, Boston College and Maryland — were ranked ahead of them in the AP poll. "I guess the secret to the poll popularity contest is that if you're going to lose games, you have better lose them early and not late,'' said Nehlen.

Nehlen was determined not to make the same mistake in bowl preparations this time that he had made for the Gator Bowl. In 1982 he took his Mountaineers to Florida nine days early. And he worked the team long and hard. "We peaked too soon for that game,'' said Nehlen. "And I had to take the blame for that.''

This time the Mountaineers' bowl practices lasted only about 50 minutes. Fifty intense minutes.

Nehlen said, "I won't say I'm that smart. What happened was when we began our bowl workouts in Morgantown, it was as cold as the dickens. We started practicing only about 50 minutes because it was so cold. And lo and behold, our kids started practicing like crazy. I couldn't believe how they were going at it. So, I told the squad, 'Men, when we go to Birmingham, we aren't going very long.' And when we got to Birmingham we never went more than 90 minutes total, from the time we stepped on the field until we walked off. Our kids were fresh and enthusiastic.''

The WVU coach did something prior to the Hall of Fame Bowl that few major college coaches in America would have done. He agreed to a newspaper contest, sponsored by the Charleston, W. Va., *Daily Mail,* in which fans would send in plays to 'Help Him Win the Bowl Game.' Nehlen selected the winning play and said he would actually use it sometime during the game.

It's unlikely that coaches at Nebraska, Texas, Oklahoma, Penn State, Ohio State, Pitt, or coaches at any of the other schools in bowls would have agreed to such a contest.

Nehlen said, "Why did I agree to do such a thing? Simple. The game of football should be fun. Life is too short to take everything so seriously. Naturally, we want to win the game. But we also want to have fun. A bowl game is a reward for the players, the coaches and fans for an outstanding season.

"I think this idea of a play contest adds a little pizzazz to the game.''

Nehlen didn't take his squad to Birmingham nine days before the bowl game this time. He took them to Birmingham on a Sunday and five days later played the game.

Nehlen did one more thing, too. He was determined that he, his coaching staff and players profit by what had happened to Florida in the 1981 Peach Bowl. "If you remember,'' said Nehlen, "we went to the Peach Bowl to play Florida, and all the talk was about how Florida was

going to kick our tails. It was Florida this, and Florida that. We weren't supposed to have a chance. And Florida came into the game a bunch of fat cats and we dominated them (26-6).

"Now, we were in the same shoes in the Hall of Fame Bowl that Florida was in the Peach Bowl. We were favored to beat Kentucky. Everything our kids read was West Virginia this, and West Virginia that. It was our turn to see if we could handle all that stuff. I know enough about the game to know that it wasn't true. Anybody you play in a bowl game is going to be a tough opponent. And I knew Jerry (Kentucky coach Jerry Claiborne) would have his kids breathing fire. I knew we'd have our hands full.''

And by Nehlen's design, a relaxed and confident West Virginia team took to the artificial turf in Birmingham's Legion Field to meet 7-4 Kentucky on a frigid Dec. 22 night. Unfortunately for the Mountaineers, Kentucky was relaxed and confident, too — and fired up. In the first half, the Mountaineers managed to score only three points, a 39-yard field goal by Paul Woodside, and trailed, 10-3.

In the locker room at halftime, Nehlen and his coaches went over first half mistakes with the players. They took time, too, to call prospective recruits and let the recruits know WVU was interested enough in them to take time out at halftime of a bowl game to talk to them.

One recruit that Nehlen talked to said, "Coach, you and your team aren't doing too well, are you?''

Nehlen said, "No, not yet. But have you got your television set on?''

The kid said, "Yes,''

Nehlen said, "Well, we've got a few things up our sleeves. Watch for the onside kick to start the second half.

Actually, the onside kick was the idea of assistant coach Bob Simmons, who years ago played linebacker for Nehlen at Bowling Green State University. Nehlen agreed and said, "What the heck, this is a bowl game. We need a lift. Let's go for it. My man Woody (placekicker Paul Woodside) can do it.''

And the Mountaineers did. Woodside hit a perfect squib kick to start the second half and recovered it himself. The play caught the Wildcats by surprise. West Virginia had possession at the Kentucky 48, and eight plays later Jeff Hostetler, who had misfired on all 10 passing attempts in the first half and was stricken with a migraine headache, lofted a pass to the corner of the end zone to Rich Hollins. Woodside kicked the extra point. The score was, 10-10, and West Virginia was back in the game.

"That onside kick gave us the lift we needed,'' said Nehlen. "We had played with great emotion up to that point, but we needed to get something going offensively. That did it.''

In the fourth quarter, Hostetler hit Rob Bennett with a nine-yard touchdown pass to give the Mountaineers a 17-10 lead. And minutes later, Woodside booted his second field goal of the game, a 23-yarder, to make it, 20-10. Kentucky went to the air in the closing minute and managed a final score, but that was all.

West Virginia won, 20-16.

Afterward, Nehlen said, "I think we gave the Hall of

Fame Bowl its money's worth. When you think of it, this has been an exciting year. Going into this season we had lost about 50 percent of our defense and 40 percent of our offense from the year before. Yet, this team came back with a 9-3 season for the third season in a row. At one time it ranked No. 4 in the country. It went to a bowl for the third straight year. No, I take that back. It's not exciting. It's fantastic.''

When all the bowl games were over and the final polls were announced, West Virginia was ranked the 16th-best team in the country, the third year in a row that the Mountaineers had finished in the top 20. A few weeks later, Nehlen was given the honor of being the head coach for the East squad in the annual East-West Shrine Game in Palo Alto, Calif. His assistants were Howard Schnellenberger, head coach of national champion Miami, and Earle Bruce, head coach of Fiesta Bowl champ Ohio State.

In four seasons, Don Nehlen had turned a losing program into a winner and — and put West Virginia, and himself, in the upper echelon of major college football. In fact, through the 1983 season his 13-year record of 86-50-4 (.632 winning percentage) as a college head coach was the 26th best among the nation's active coaches.

Michigan Coach Bo Schembechler, the man Nehlen credits for furthering his education as a football coach, said of Nehlen, "It was a real coup for West Virginia when it hired Don Nehlen as its head coach. As long as Don Nehlen stays at West Virginia, West Virginia is going to be a very, very good football team.''

Nehlen laughed and said, "Bo is being very kind. Why have we won? I don't know. We've worked hard, but I don't know of a coach in America who doesn't work hard. Maybe we've been lucky.

"We've won a few games here at West Virginia University and Mountaineer fans think I'm special.

"That's ridiculous. I'm nobody special.''

Chapter Sixteen

(Editor's note: The following, unless otherwise noted, is West Virginia University head coach Don Nehlen talking about his coaching philosophy.)

You know, I don't profess to know an awfully lot about the game of football, because I'm not that smart. But I think I know something about winning.

I once was quoted as saying I was the best coach in America. I don't remember saying that. But it doesn't really matter how good I am. What matters is how good I think I am. And I think I'm pretty good. I believe I'm the best. That's all that counts.

The same holds true for my players. I don't care how good they are. I do care how good they think they are. If they think they're the best, then we'll get it done.

First of all, we operate under the family concept at West Virginia University, not only as a coaching staff, but as a football team. I'm the head of the team. Therefore, I'm the head of the family. And all those players are my pups.

The family concept is very important, because I've found that the family that's close is tough to beat.

Family has always been important to me. That really hit home when my wife, Merry Ann, had that heart attack (Jan. 16, 1984). She's doing fine now. But when it happened, I couldn't believe it. I was afraid she might not make it. But I refused to even think about what my life would be like without Merry Ann. After that my priorities changed a little.

When I was a young coach, I used to go to work at 7 a.m. and not get home until 1 a.m. or 2 a.m. I don't do that anymore.

I try to help out around the house more than I used to. And going on vacation is more important than it used to be. Going out on the boat with Merry Ann is more important than it used to be.

Now, don't get me wrong. Coaching football is still awfully high on my list. That's why I feel so strongly about my coaching philosophy.

I have a definite way of dealing with my assistant coaches. I give them an area of responsibility and hold them accountable for it. I don't interfere with their daily, on-the-field coaching. It is up to each coach to go out on the field and use his own drills and individuality to teach players at the certain position he is coaching, and bring them to where we want them to be.

We talk constantly about how to handle our players. That's the only part of coaching I will interfere with. I won't interfere with the coaching on the field — that is,

unless I don't like it.

Now, if I don't like the way an individual coach is coaching, I'll call him into my office and say, "Hey, that's not what I want."

And that's happened a few times since I've been at West Virginia.

I've fired only one coach since I've been coaching. And I did it because he wasn't teaching the players what I wanted taught. You gotta understand, I expect my coaches to do their jobs, and do them the way I want them done. If they don't, then I'm going to make a change.

For instance, I don't want my coaches hassling the players and getting them all ticked off. If my coaches don't have good morale with their little groups of players, what in the heck am I going to do to improve morale when I blow the whistle and call the squad all together?

My coaches know I would never ask them to do anything I wouldn't do myself. And I don't care if it means working 30 hours a week, 60 hours a week, 80 hours a week, or 100 hours a week. We work until the job is done.

I guess you could call my coaching a throwback to Woody Hayes (former Ohio State coach). I learned my coaching under Doyt Perry at Bowling Green and Bo Schembechler at Michigan. Both are disciples of Hayes. And I'm not talking about three yards and a cloud of dust coaching. I'm talking about a sound, disciplined football program.

Perry and Schembechler have had the most influence on me by a country mile in everything I do. So, when I came to West Virginia, I knew exactly what I wanted to do and how I wanted to do it. I knew who I wanted to hire as assistant coaches and what I wanted them doing.

Now, I believe the No. 1 characteristic of all good head football coaches is that they are a little bit unpredictable.

Am I unpredictable?

I am now.

When I coached at Bowling Green, I was one of the best organized coaches in America. I was organized to the nth degree because that's what I thought it took to win. I had agendas for meetings and everything would be listed 1-2-3-4-5 — right down the line. My coaches had copies of my agenda prior to each meeting and knew exactly what I was going to do. So did my players. Everything was down in black and white.

As I look back, those meetings were probably pretty boring. And I was probably just an average football coach at best.

I don't do that stuff any more. Now when I go into a meeting I might have a few things listed 1-2-3-4. There are things that I want my coaches to know about, and know exactly what's going on. But there are certain areas where I don't want them to know. Let them find out on their own.

Let them think, "What's this guy Nehlen doing?"

When I go into a team meeting I want my players thinking, "I wonder what he's going to do next?"

There has to be a separation between me and my coaches and me and my players. That unpredictability creates that separation. Now, what else does that do? Well, it keeps everyone on his toes. My coaches are never sitting around doing nothing. Things are always happening around here. And one of the reasons is because the old man who runs the ship is a little unpredictable.

I remember after I finished reading the book about Bear Bryant, I thought, "Nobody ever knew what they guy was going to do." It's the same with Schembechler. No one at Michigan is quite sure what he's going to do next, either.

Now, as far as the football goes, I'm well-organized. It's the little day-to-day things I'm talking about.

Has it made me a better football coach? I don't know. I don't know what makes good coaches, or what makes bad coaches. But I do know I have good relationships with my coaches. They trust me. They know I'll go to bat for them. Yet, they also know I'm the boss.

I'm a friend to my players, too. I like my players. But I'm not buddy-buddy with them. There has to be a separation. I don't call my players into my office just to shoot the bull with them.

But I do have an open-door policy. Anytime I go into a meeting or a conference, I tell my secretary that I don't want to be disturbed, unless it's one of my players. My players come first with me. They are the most important people in this program, because without them we have nothing. My players know that and know they can come and see me because my door is always open.

Now, they don't come to see me unless it's something pretty important. I suppose some of them are a little afraid of me.

I firmly believe a head coach has to be unpredictable to maintain the kind of discipline you have to have to have a winning program.

I'm not the kind of guy who wants a program where the players are afraid to move around. I'm not interested in a military type program where the kids don't have any fun.

I tell my kids, "We operate in a certain framework. But when you get outside that framework, then you have a problem."

But I will not put the squeeze on my players until they dislike the program. I have a saying that I repeat all the time to my kids, "Hey, man, I don't want to hassle you. And I don't want you to hassle me."

I have a certain way of establishing relationships with my coaches' wives, too. When I hire an assistant, I want to talk to his wife. I want Merry Ann to talk to her, too. I want that coach's wife to understand that if her husband takes the job I'm offering, that it isn't going to be a great job. I want the wives to know that their husbands are going to work long hours.

Now, we do a lot of things together as a staff. We have picnics and outings in the summer. We do things together on Saturday nights after home games. And when we recruit, the wives help us when we entertain the recruits. There are quite a few functions for the wives, and quite a few they are expected to attend.

For instance, when we bring a recruit and his mom and dad in, I expect that mom to have another woman to talk to. That's where the wives come in. It can't be Merry Ann all the time. My coaches' wives understand that they contribute to the success of our football program.

And I go out of my way to see that the wives are treated fairly. When we go to a bowl, the wives get bowl watches. And when the wives travel with us, they get per diem.

I fight hard for the people who work for me.

I'm not satisfied with my coaches' salaries, but we're moving in the right direction. My coaches are paid competitive wages. Now, I'm sure there are assistants in the country making more money. But I know that there are assistants out there making less money, too.

We're working on those salaries. Good assistant coaches are hard to find. And since we've won, a lot of people are interested in our coaches. To have a winning program, you have to have a little bit of consistency on your coaching staff. You can't hire a new line coach or a new quarterback coach every year. Since I've been here we've been very fortunate. We've lost just three coaches. One — Gary Tranquill — is now the head coach at Navy. Another — Carl Battershell — is an assistant at Arizona State. And another — Bill McConnnell — went into professional football with the Pittsburgh Maulers of the United States Football League.

I know I'm going to lose coaches, but I don't want to lose coaches just because somebody will pay them $5,000 or $6,000 more a year. I want my coaches paid well enough so they aren't looking to go somewhere else, and so that when someone does hire one away from us that he goes as a head coach, or an extremely high-paid assistant head coach.

I don't want my assistant coaches to leave West Virginia just because we don't treat them right.

My philosophy in regard to disciplining players has changed. For example, when I coached at Bowling Green, if I had a good player who was in trouble and I had to discipline him, or I had one who was about to flunk out, that just killed me. I would say, "Oh, my gosh, how can we play without that guy? He's one of our best players."

Today that doesn't even bother me. There's not one single football player on our team that we can't play without.

If one flunks out, that's unfortunate. If I have to kick one off the team, that's too bad. But I'd do it and not even worry about it.

When I was a young coach, I thought we had to have all our players all the time. I remember at Bowling Green I had a great linebacker named Phil Villapiano (who went on to be all-pro with the Oakland Raiders).

I loved that kid, but boy, did I have trouble with him. Finally, he backed me into a corner. I called him in and said, "Phil, if I hear of you getting into any more trouble, you're gone." I called his dad on the phone and told him the same thing.

Not too long after that, I got word through the grapevine that there had been a big fight in the dormitory and that Phil was in the middle of it tossing people and furniture around. So, I told my equipment man to take his uniform out of his locker. That was it.

The next day before practice, there was a knock on my office door. I said, "Who is it?"

I heard his voice say, "It's Phil, coach."

I said, "Come on in."

He asked, "Where is my uniform, coach? It's not in my locker."

I said, "I had it taken up. You know what I told you. I warned you about getting into any more trouble."

He said, "Coach, I didn't do anything this time. All I did was try to break up the fight. Honest. I was the only good guy there."

I laughed and said, "Yeah, I know all about how good you've been, Phil."

Anyhow, Vallapiano went and got the dean of students, a man named Ray Whittaker. And a few hours later, here came Villapiano and the dean marching out on the practice field. The dean said to me, "Don, you won't believe this, but Phil didn't do a thing. He has been guilty of a lot of things, but he wasn't guilty last night."

And that was the last problem I had with Phil Villapiano. He was a special breed. He made my life interesting, but I loved him.

Having to discipline Phil bothered me. Today that wouldn't bother me at all. I've learned through trial and error how to handle the players. I've learned not to have a lot of rules, because then you have to enforce them. I don't want to enforce rules.

I don't even have a rule that my players can't drink alcohol. I'm not a hypocrite. I know where my guys go on Saturday night. I know what goes on, on a college campus. I wasn't born yesterday.

I tell my players, "Hey, you guys are 20 and 21 years old. Some of you are married and have children. For me to tell you that you can't have a bottle would be hypocritical.

"If you want to take your girl and go downtown where the fun is, that's fine. That's part of growing up. And if you want to have a beer, that's fine. But if you have eight or 10 beers and get into a fight and embarrass the program, that's different. You're out the door. And if having a beer affects your performance, you have a problem. And I guarantee you, I will handle that problem.

"And for me to tell you that you can't smoke a cigarette would be hypocritical. However, I don't smoke and I think you're stupid if you do. If you want to smoke, I can't stop you. But if one of you is seen walking down the street smoking a cigarette by me or one of my coaches, you are automatically dropped from the squad.

"If you're stupid enough to want to smoke, I don't give a darn. Just do it in private. You can put them in both ears and in both nostrils for all I care. But if you do it in public and embarrass the program, you're gone. And if it affects your performance, I'll handle that, too."

Like I said, I don't want rules on my team. I want attitudes. I want a strength attitude. I want an attitude that my kids want to stay out of bars and leave cigarettes alone because they want to win.

I want an attitude where my kids say, "Hey, for my own good health I'm not going to do that stuff."

The feeling I want my players to understand is that if they act like men, I'll treat them like men. And if they act like bums, I'll treat them like bums.

I think the big difference in my handling of players is that I'm secure jobwise. When I coached at Bowling Green I wasn't secure. I believe very strongly that today in coaching the key to the very successful head coach, besides that unpredictability I mentioned earlier, is for the coach to get a contract where he doesn't have to worry about little decisions that might put him in a bad light.

I don't have to worry about my job at West Virginia. When Dick Martin (then WVU athletic director) hired me, he said he would give me a four-year contract. I said, "Dick, you're going to give me a five-year contract. You've had four losing seasons. The program is down. I don't know if I can get it done in four years. I may need that fifth year."

Anyhow, my initial contract was for four years. At the end of the first year, another year was added to it. And at the end of every year since, the contract has just been rolled over. So, I always have a four-year contract. That's about as much security as any football coach can have. Personally, I think I have the best coaching contract in the country.

Now, I don't make near the money a lot of coaches make. My base salary is $50,300. But my television show has improved a heckuva lot. We have access to a nice cottage on Tygart Lake. We recently bought a condominum in Florida.

My salary may not be as high as some of my coaching friends. But it's not too bad. And the people of West Virginia have been so nice to Merry Ann and me. That's worth more than money. Besides, if you don't have the love of God, your health and the love of your family, what good is money? Money means nothing if you don't have that. All it does is make life a little nicer. And it is nice to go to the grocery store and buy ground chuck instead of ground beef.

Like I said, I don't have to worry about my job. I don't have to worry about going 9-3 every year. So, if I have to make a tough decision, one that's going to cost us a game or two, but help the program over the long haul, I'll go ahead and make it.

But when a coach is scratching from year to year, things are different. For instance, I wouldn't have made a tough decision that might have cost me a game at Bowling Green. No way. I wasn't secure in my job there.

When a person is totally in charge, he does what's

right for the total program all the time, and doesn't worry about the little things. When a guy is hanging on by a one-year contract, he doesn't coach as well. And he certainly can't be himself.

That's one of the things an administrator doesn't understand. An administrator would be much better off giving a coach a four- or five-year contract and say to the coach, "Do it your way." The school would get a much better performance.

Besides, if a coach can't do it in four or five years, chances are he isn't going to do it at all.

But the big difference in my coaching is confidence. Strictly confidence. And that came from Bo Schembechler, and from three years I spent in one of the finest football programs in the country. I was able to compare what I did at one job (Bowling Green) to what was done at Michigan. And I discovered what I had done at the other job wasn't all that bad.

I mentioned earlier about my open-door policy with my players. That coach-player relationship is very important. When my players say they need to see me, I know it must be very important or they wouldn't bother me.

You can't have 100 kids on a team without having a death in one of the kid's family. We have two or three deaths a year. Some of the kids' parents, or brothers or sisters, will get seriously ill. Sometimes, a best friend will die in an accident. Sometimes, a girlfriend will get an illness that is terminal.

I remember one year we had a player whose father died, his grandmother died and his mother went on unemployment — all in the space of two months.

Something like that is catastrophic to anyone, and especially to a 19- or 20-year-old.

And you can't get through a year without four or five of your kids getting a girlfriend pregnant. That's the truth. And I don't care whether it's Bethany, Bowling Green, Michigan, West Virginia, or wherever.

Those are problems that the players need to talk to somebody about. Maybe I don't solve them, but I listen.

Too many coaches don't listen. When a player comes in to see him, the coach will want to talk about how the player is doing on the strength program, how much he weighs, how much weight he has gained, etc. All of a sudden, all the kid is doing is answering questions.

And he's the one who came in to see the coach. And the coach didn't have time to listen.

One thing I've learned over the long haul is that when a kid comes into my office, I tell myself, "Shut up, Don. Shut up, and listen. Just sit still and listen to what the kid has to say."

When I was a young coach and a kid came in to see me, I monopolized the meeting. And I'm sure the kid walked out of my office and thought, "Gee, I never got to tell him what my problem was." Now, when I was doing that, I thought I was doing a good job. But I wasn't.

The thing that's tough for a coach to swallow is that football is not the only thing in a student-athlete's life. He has academics. He has girlfriends. He has dormitory life. He has fraternities. He has a mom, dad, brothers, sisters

and grandparents at home.

And along the way, the kid will play football, too.

If a coach just tries to zero in on football as the only common ground he has with his players, he's making a mistake, a terrible mistake.

I'm good at establishing relationships along lines other than football with my players now. Ten years ago I wasn't good at that. Basically, the important thing I've learned is to listen.

Now, aside from the open-door policy and having an ear, the next thing you have to have with your kids is honesty. I preach that to my players all the time.

I say, "Hey, man, it's very difficult for me to be your coach, to be your teacher, to be a person who can help you with your problems, if I can't trust you. One thing you have to understand is that I will never lie to you. And I don't want you to lie to me."

I have never lied to a football player since the day I walked in here.

Now, have I ever lied to a football player? I would answer that by saying, "Not intentionally." But as a young coach I had a tendency to tell some of my players what they wanted to hear. I wasn't totally honest. But I don't think I ever purposely lied. I just kind of appeased them.

Ten years ago, if a player had walked into my office and asked, "What do I have to do to make the team, coach?" I would have answered, "Well, you have to gain 15 pounds. You have to get faster. You have to get stronger." I would have said that even though deep in my heart I knew the kid didn't have a chance to play.

Now, if a kid asks me that question, I say, "I don't think you're going to make this team. If I told you if you worked all summer that you'd have a chance to make the team, I'd be lying to you. I won't lie to you. I don't think you can play."

Most kids don't like to hear that. But that's exactly what I tell them. I'm as honest as I can possibly be.

The other thing I do in my relationships with the players is tell them that since the team is a family, whenever there's a problem, we bring it to the family. Now, I'm not going to bring up something in front of the team that would embarass a kid. I'm not going to bring up that a kid's father has died, or that he has a girl pregnant, or something like that.

But when I discipline a player for anything, I tell the entire team what I'm doing. And I tell the player I'm disciplining, "You have to understand that I'm going to tell the entire team that I'm disciplining you."

That way I can't back out.

When I discipline a kid, I tell the team. "I'm having a problem with this guy. I want all of you to know what I told him."

For instance, we once had a player who had been getting into trouble in bars. I called the kid in and told him, "If I hear of you setting one foot in one more bar, your behind is off this squad."

And I told the team, particularly the seniors, "And if you guys see him in a bar and don't tell me, then we're going to lose. If you don't tell me, we have no chance of winning because we won't have honesty. Understand, I'll find out anyway. And I'll still drop the guy from the squad. Do you guys understand where I'm coming from?''

Hey, if my seniors don't tell me, then I have to wonder about my seniors.

When you handle discipline that way, the entire team knows you're not bluffing. And it puts an awful lot of pressure on the particular kid being disciplined, and an awful lot of responsibility on your seniors. But I expect my seniors to be leaders off the field, too.

And that brings my philosophy around to senior leadership. That is something every team has to have. It is vital. I tell my players they have to understand that the seniors are special. They are more important than the freshmen, more important than the sophomores, and more important than the juniors. And then I list the reasons.

I say, ''The seniors are important because they've been here. They've gone through the program. They are part of us. And if we win, they will be the biggest reasons why we win. And if we lose, they'll be the biggest reasons why we lose.''

Every year I fully expect our seniors to have their greatest years. And if they don't, then we have no chance of winning.

And then I single out each senior in front of the team and challenge each one. I single them all out, even a fourth-team quarterback, if he happens to be a senior. I say to the fourth-teamer, ''If you're not the best fourth-team quarterback in America this year, then we have no chance of winning.''

I have about five meetings a year with my seniors. I bring them into the meeting room in my office and talk with them about the team and what we are doing. I think it's important that your seniors know how to win.

A lot of head coaches think that if they have good players on their teams they'll win. Good players do have a lot to do with winning, but there are lots of teams every year with good players that lose.

Those teams lose because they don't understand the mechanism of winning. They don't understand the importance of attitude, of loyalty, of honesty, of discipline, of senior leadership. Those are the things that win for you.

As a coach, I seldom get up in front of the team and diagram a play. Now, I'll get up in front of the coaching staff and diagram plays. But I don't do that in front of the team. I don't waste any time. Besides, we teach on the part, part, whole method. I know that my tight end coach has taught the tight ends their assignments on the '56 play.' I know that my tackle and guard coaches have taught the tackles and guards their assignments. Then, it's just a matter of putting the pieces together.

When I get up in front of the team, I talk to them about what it takes to win. I don't want to waste my time diagraming our 56 play.

Now, putting the pieces of the plays together will just get you though a game. It won't win for you. It's my job to make sure the team understands the mechanism of winning.

For example, at one recent team meeting, we went over our team goals. I said, ''If I asked you to go over three things that have to happen in order for us to win, what would be No. 1?''

One player held up his hand and said, ''Senior leadership, coach.''

I said, ''Why?''

He said, ''Because no great team ever wins without senior leadership.''

Now, I know the kid said that because he had heard me say it 1,000 times. But that tells me I've stamped it on his mind.

I expect that if my senior class is worth a nickel, then I won't have morale problems.

I want my players to be concerned only with the team. We have to all be going in the same direction. And we have to all go with no one caring who gets the credit.

The defense doesn't win. The offense doesn't win. The quarterback doesn't win. The field goal kicker doesn't win. Don Nehlen doesn't win.

West Virginia wins.

We all win, or we all lose.

Any coach who has been around the game of football for X number of years can go out on the practice field and teach a team how to play the game. I mean, you have to have ends, tackles, guards, quarterbacks, running backs, linebackers, defensive backs.

But there's a difference between playing and winning. And I'm telling you it's between the ears. It's in the mind.

When I coached at Bowling Green, we spent hours and hours running the 56 play, the 10 trap, all that stuff. Heck, I was smart enough, even back then, to have a good offense. And I knew how to come up with a defense. And I thought that's what it took to win.

Oh, sure, a team has to know how to run the plays. But the plays don't win for you. It's the attitude, intensity and morale of the 11 guys you have on the field that win for you. You win with players who have the will to prepare themselves to win. All players want to win. Few want to prepare to win.

And the big part of my job is to motivate the players so they want to do that. I never stop motivating. I've always felt one of my strengths as a coach is in the area of motivation.

When you think of motivation you have to think of four areas: (1) self-image, (2) security, (3) challenge, and (4) recognition.

Understand, I'm talking about football. My players already know the No. 1 reason they're at West Virginia is to get an education. They know that we will do everything in our power to give them the tools so they can graduate. Most of them will graduate. A few won't. But we have no more control over the few who don't than we do over the kid who insists in hanging out in a bar. My kids know how I feel about education.

In motivating, you start with a player's self-image. I don't think you can motivate a football player, or any other individual, unless he has a good image of himself. A person who has a bad self-image is the person who's walk-